Trade in Counterfeit Goods and the Italian Economy

PROTECTING ITALY'S INTELLECTUAL PROPERTY

This work is published under the responsibility of the Secretary-General of the OECD. The opinions expressed and arguments employed herein do not necessarily reflect the official views of OECD member countries.

This document, as well as any data and any map included herein, are without prejudice to the status of or sovereignty over any territory, to the delimitation of international frontiers and boundaries and to the name of any territory, city or area.

Please cite this publication as:
OECD (2018), *Trade in Counterfeit Goods and the Italian Economy: Protecting Italy's intellectual property*, OECD Publishing, Paris.
http://dx.doi.org/10.1787/9789264302426-en

ISBN 978-92-64-30241-9 (print)
ISBN 978-92-64-30242-6 (PDF)

The statistical data for Israel are supplied by and under the responsibility of the relevant Israeli authorities. The use of such data by the OECD is without prejudice to the status of the Golan Heights, East Jerusalem and Israeli settlements in the West Bank under the terms of international law.

Photo credits: Cover © Jeffrey Fisher.

Corrigenda to OECD publications may be found on line at: *www.oecd.org/about/publishing/corrigenda.htm*.

Preface

The Italian economy is innovative, knowledge-intense and globalised. Numerous Italian industries produce high-quality products that are highly valued and in demand around the world. These features are the hallmarks of a modern, dynamic economy; however, they also make Italy vulnerable to the global risks of counterfeiting and piracy.

To deal with these risks in an effective way, we need more information on their scale, scope and impact. This study assesses the effects of trade in counterfeit goods on the Italian industry, government and consumers. It does so from two perspectives: first, it examines the scale of counterfeit and pirated products smuggled into Italy; second, it looks at the scale and effects of global trade in counterfeit goods that infringe on the rights of Italian trademark holders.

We are confident this report will contribute to a better understanding of the risk that counterfeiting poses for Italy, and will assist policy makers in formulating effective solutions to combat this scourge.

Loredana Gulino
DG For the Fight Against Counterfeiting –
Italian Patent and Trademark Office
Ministry of Economic Development

Marcos Bonturi
Director,
OECD, Public Governance Directorate

Foreword

Italy produces high valued products and benefits significantly from its intellectual property and trademarks. It is also well integrated in the global economy, through active participation in global value chains. This makes it particularly susceptible to the damaging effects of counterfeiting and piracy.

The risk of trade in counterfeits has been growing in recent years. It not only poses a significant threat to the engine of economic growth, but also undermines good governance, the rule of law and citizens' trust in government. As shown by the recent OECD reports, *Trade in Counterfeit and Pirated Goods: Mapping the Economic Impact and Mapping the Real Routes of Trade in Fake Goods*, trade in counterfeit and pirated goods amounted to up to 2.5 % of world trade in 2013, and made up an even higher share (5%) of imports into the EU. Parties that engage in counterfeit trade are well organised, and ship goods via very complex routes that pose a formidable challenge for enforcement authorities.

Trade in counterfeit goods damages Italian rights holders, the Italian government, and Italian consumers. This report measures the direct economic effects of counterfeiting on consumers, retail and manufacturing industries, and government. It assesses both the impact of imports of fake products to Italy and the impact of the global trade in fake products on Italian intellectual property rights holders.

This study was carried out by the OECD's Task Force on Countering Illicit Trade. The Task Force is part of the OECD High Level Risk Forum, which focuses on evidence-based research and advanced analytics to assist policy makers in mapping and understanding the market vulnerabilities exploited and created by illicit trade. This is the first of a set of country and regional case studies that will not only assess the scale and magnitude of counterfeit trade, but also quantify some of its negative economic impacts at a regional level.

The report was prepared by Piotr Stryszowski, Senior Economist, and Florence Mouradian, Economist at the OECD Directorate for Public Governance and Territorial Development, under the supervision of Stéphane Jacobzone, Counsellor, OECD.

The authors wish to thank Francesca Cappiello and Paola Riccio from the Italian the Ministry of Economic Development for their co-operation, and useful insights.

The authors are grateful to participants of several seminars and workshops for the valuable assistance provided. Special expressions of appreciation are given to Mr. Edoardo Mazzilli from the Italian Custom Agency, Mr. Claudio Bergonzi from Indicam, as well as to Mr. Alessandro Farris and Mr. Stefano Orsini from Luxottica.

The OECD Secretariat wishes to thank Liv Gaunt, Randy Holden and Andrea Uhrhammer for their editorial and production support.

The quantitative research in this study relied on the customs database provided by the World Customs Organization (WCO). It was supplemented with regional data submitted by the European Commission's Directorate-General for Taxation and Customs Union, the US Customs and Border Protection Agency and the US Immigration and Customs Enforcement. In addition, some statistical information was also drawn from the rich the IPERICO database on seizures done in Italy, provided by the Italian Ministry of Economic Development. The authors express their gratitude for the data and for the valuable support of these institutions.

Table of contents

Tables

Figures

Boxes

Acronyms and Abbreviations

BEPS	Base Erosion and Profit Shifting programme (OECD)
CbC	Country-by-country (reporting)
CEN	Customs Enforcement Network
CIT	Corporate income tax
DGLC-UIBM	Direzione Generale Lotta alla Contraffazione - Ufficio Italiano Brevetti e Marchi (Directorate-General for the Fight Against Counterfeiting – Italian Patent and Trademark Office)
EUIPO	European Union Intellectual Property Office
GTRIC-e	General Trade-Related Index of Counterfeiting for economies
GTRIC-p	General Trade-Related Index of Counterfeiting for ICT products
IMPACT	International Medical Products Anti-Counterfeiting Taskforce
IP	Intellectual property
IPERICO	Intellectual Property – Elaborated Report of the Investigation on Counterfeiting database
mn	Million(s)
NACE	Nomenclature statistique des activités économiques dans la Communauté européenne (Statistical classification of economic activities in the European Community)
n.e.c.	Not classified elsewhere
OLAF	Office européen de lutte antifraude (European Anti-Fraud Office)
PIT	Personal income taxes
R&D	Research and development
RAS	Rapid Alert System
SSC	Social security contributions
VAT	Value-added taxes
WCO	World Customs Organization
WHO	World Health Organization

Executive summary

Trade in counterfeit goods is a longstanding, worldwide socio-economic problem that is growing in scope and magnitude. It challenges effective governance, efficient business and the well-being of consumers, even as it becomes a key source of income for organised criminal groups.

For consumers, counterfeiting poses dangers to health, safety and privacy. It may also lower consumer satisfaction, notably when low-quality fake goods are purchased unknowingly. For rights holders and their authorised vendors, rising counterfeiting increases revenue losses, while trademark infringements continuously erode brands' value. For governments, counterfeiting means lost tax revenues, higher unemployment and greater expenses incurred – both to ensure compliance with anti-counterfeiting legislation, and to react to public safety threats and labour market distortions.

This report presents the findings of the Italy case study of trade in counterfeit and pirated goods. It examines the scale of counterfeit and pirated products smuggled into Italy, and the effect on consumers, industries and the Italian government, as well as the scale and effects of global trade in counterfeit goods that infringe on the rights of Italian trademark holders. This dual analysis is based primarily on a quantitative assessment of global trade in counterfeit products within and outside the Italian economy, using a rich database on seizures of counterfeit products, compiled from various sources. The findings can help both public and private sector decision makers better understand the nature and scale of the problem for the Italian economy, and develop appropriate, cohesive and evidence-based policy responses.

Key findings

- The best estimates indicate that counterfeit and pirated imports in Italy accounted for as much as EUR 10.4 billion in 2013 – the equivalent of 3% of Italian imports in genuine goods.
- The degree of counterfeiting in Italy varies considerably across product categories. In absolute terms, ICT devices were the most counterfeited type of goods, with an estimated value of EUR 2.3 billion of fakes imported in Italy in 2013. In relative terms, articles of leather and handbags, toys and games, and clothing were most targeted by counterfeiters, with fakes accounting for 15.3%, 14.3% and 13.4%, respectively, of Italian imports from these product categories.
- The analysis shows that around half of imported counterfeit and pirated goods in Italy in 2013 were sold to consumers who actually knew they were buying fake products, with the remaining share purchased unwittingly. The share of fakes bought knowingly in Italy varies significantly by product, ranging from 15% for foodstuff to 60% for watches and ICT devices.
- Available data show global trade in counterfeit and pirated products that infringed Italian trademarks amounted to as much as EUR 35.6 billion in 2013, equivalent to 4.9% of total Italian manufacturing sales (domestic plus exports).

- Sectors where Italian IPR were particularly targeted, in terms of the absolute value of trade, include (i) electronic, electrical equipment and optical products; (ii) clothing, footwear, and leather articles; and (iii) foodstuff. As a percentage of total trade in a given product category, clothing, footwear, leather articles; electronic, electrical and optical products, and perfumery and cosmetics, were the types of Italian products most often faked worldwide.
- Counterfeit and pirated goods that infringe the intellectual property rights (IPRs) of Italian right holders come mainly from Turkey, China and Hong Kong, China.
- The results indicate that between 2011 and 2013, over half of the goods traded worldwide that infringed Italian IPRs were offered on primary markets – that is, they were sold to unsuspecting consumers who believed they were buying genuine goods. This share varies among product categories, ranging from 32% for jewellery and watches to 85% for foodstuffs.

Impact on Italy

- The estimates for consumer detriment – that is, the price premium unjustly paid by consumers in the belief they are buying a genuine product – in Italy due to deception on primary markets in 2013 amounted to almost EUR 2 billion.
- The total volume of forgone sales in the Italian wholesalers and retailers due to counterfeit and pirated products smuggled in Italy was EUR 6.9 billion in 2013. This is equivalent to 2.7% of total sales in the Italian wholesale and retail sector in that year.
- The total volume of Italian companies' forgone sales due to infringement of their IP rights in global trade amounted to EUR 25.1 billion, or 3.1% of total sales of these Italian companies in that year (domestic plus exports).
- Lower sales reduce the demand for labour. Job losses in Italy that inevitably result in the retail and wholesale sector due to counterfeit and pirated imports totalled over 23 thousand in 2013, equivalent to more than 1.3% of all people employed in the sector. The total number of jobs lost in Italian industries due to the global infringement of their trademarks amounted to over 64 thousand, equivalent to 2.4% of the total number of employees in the Italian manufacturing sector.

  Altogether, at least 87 500 jobs were lost due to counterfeiting and piracy. That represents 2% of full time equivalent employees in Italy.
- Lower sales due to the counterfeiting markets in Italy mean lower revenues for the Italian government from value-added tax (VAT), corporate income tax (CIT), personal income tax and social security contributions.

  In 2013, forgone tax revenues from the retail and wholesale sector amounted to EUR 3.7 billion. That same year, forgone tax revenue from Italian right holders to the Italian government amounted to EUR 5.9 billion.

  Altogether, trade in counterfeit and pirated goods resulted in a reduction in Italian public revenues equal to almost EUR 10 billion, the equivalent of 1% of the taxes collected on value-added, personal and corporate incomes, and social security contributions, or 0.6% of Italian GDP.

1. Gauging the scale and effects of counterfeiting and piracy

This chapter lays the methodological groundwork for the study. It places in both quantitative and relative perspective the reliance of the Italian economy on IP, as well as the considerable damage caused by infringement. It goes on to introduce two distinctions: that between counterfeit products smuggled into Italy and IPR infringements on Italian right holders; and that between primary and secondary markets for counterfeit and pirated goods. The chapter concludes by outlining the seven categories of effects of this illicit trade, each of which will be examined in detail in the discussion that follows.

Throughout the world, intellectual property (IP) has been a driving force behind economic growth, high-paying jobs, economic competitiveness, innovation, and creative expression. IP also provides the incentive to create, invest in, and commercialise new inventions, products and services, while supporting artists and authors in disseminating their works.

Alongside this remarkably positive story of economic growth, ingenuity and creativity, however, there is the far less positive story of IP theft and the harm it does. It is essential to understand the threats posed, both at the macro level – their global scope and magnitude – and at the micro level – the nature of the complex schemes used by illicit actors to accomplish IP theft on a commercial scale. Without that understanding, and a firm grasp of the impediments to effective IP enforcement, developing and implementing an effective strategy to tackle these threats is practically impossible.

The entire Italian economy relies on some form of IP, as recent quantitative studies have shown OHIM (2013). Virtually every industry either produces or uses it, which means the Italian economy is characterised by an IPR intensity far above the EU average. In 2010, IPR-intensive industries contributed to 40.8% of Italian GDP and 26.8% of employment in Italy. With respect to trademarks only, the country ranks fourth in the EU in terms of the total number of trademarks registered during that same year; Italian trademark-intensive industries contributed to 36.1% of Italian GDP, and 21.5% of Italian total employment. These important industries rely on the recognition and effective protection of a variety of intangible assets and products of the human intellect.

Italian IPR-intensive industries are highly globalised, which contributes to their being a major driver of the country's economic growth. The Italian economy is an active participant in global value chains: in 2009, the country's exports represented 3.8% of total world exports in value added terms, which is slightly above Italy's share in gross exports and imports OECD (2013). Numerous Italian IPR-intensive industries actively participate in global value chains through exports in manufacturing, by sourcing intermediates from abroad. These include industries such as chemicals, machinery, electrical equipment and textiles.

The high IPR and trademark intensity of the Italian economy, combined with its high degree of integration within the global economy, highlights the potential for damage caused by counterfeiting and piracy, and calls for hard analysis of the phenomenon. This is especially relevant when the threats of counterfeiting and piracy[1] are growing worldwide OECD/EUIPO (2016).

Italy is one of the countries whose companies are most affected by global counterfeiting and piracy. In fact, according to OECD/EUIPO (2016), Italy ranks number two on the list of economies whose rights holders suffer from counterfeiting, directly after the United States and ahead of France, Switzerland, Japan, Germany and the United Kingdom (see Figure 1.1).

Figure 1.1. Top economies of origin of right holders whose IP rights are infringed, 2011-13

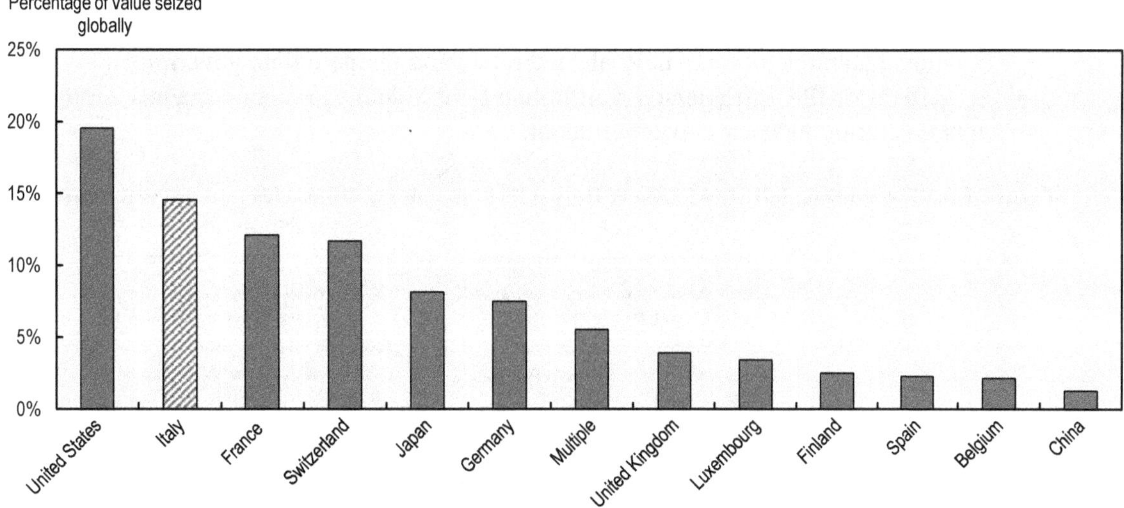

Notes: The term "multiple" refers to seizures of IP-infringing products for which right holders are registered in multiple economies. Data are based on the value of global customs seizures of counterfeit and pirated products from 2011 to 2013.
Source: OECD/EUIPO (2016).

At the same time, the OECD/EUIPO (2016) report shows that some 2.4% of the total value of counterfeit and pirated world imports was shipped to Italy between 2011 and 2013. This ranks Italy as the seventh destination economy in the world for counterfeit and pirated products (Figure 1.2).

Figure 1.2. Top destination economies for counterfeit and pirated products, 2011-13

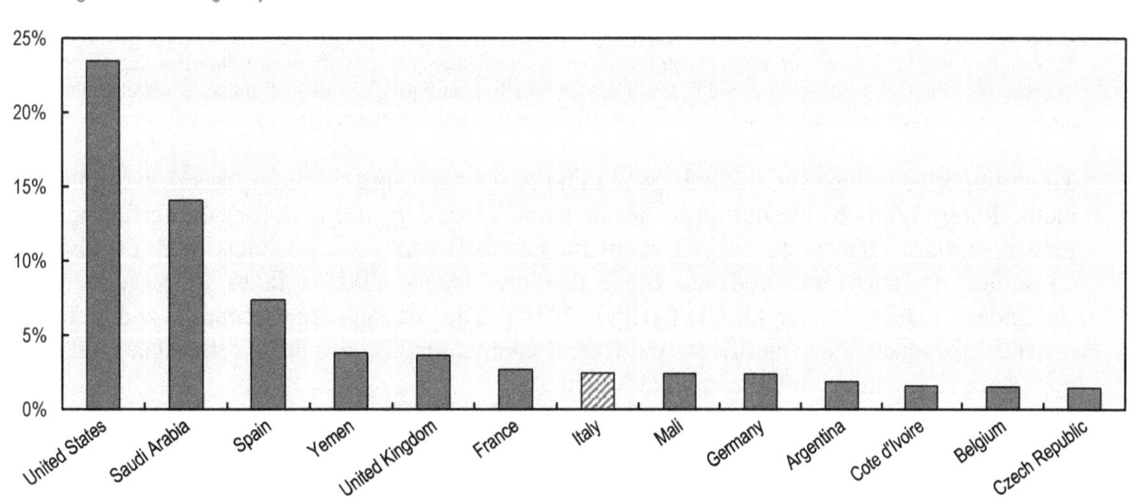

Note: Data are based on the value of global customs seizures of counterfeit and pirated products from 2011 to 2013.
Source: OECD/EUIPO (2016).

The effects of the global trade in counterfeit goods on the Italian economy can be assessed from two perspectives (see Figure 1.3):

- the effects of counterfeit products smuggled into Italy on consumers; industries, including manufacturing, wholesale and retail; and on the Italian government
- the effects of IPR infringements on Italian right holders, and consequently on the manufacturing industry and government.

Figure 1.3. How counterfeit trade affects Italy – its consumers, industries and government

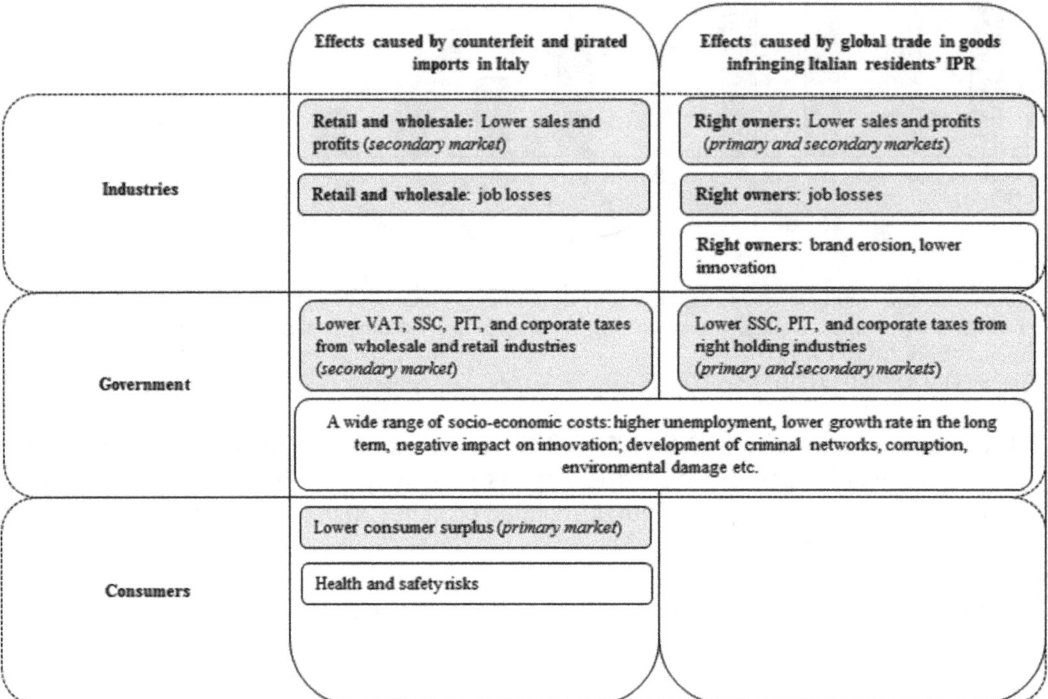

Notes: Grey indicates areas for which quantitative analysis of impact is possible (with varying degrees of robustness in the final results). White indicates areas for which quantitative analysis of impact is not currently possible. VAT refers to value-added taxes, SSC to social security contributions, PIT to personal income taxes.

Three important things should be kept in mind when analysing these impacts. Firstly, the methodology refers to the notion of *primary and secondary markets* for counterfeit and pirated goods. That is to say, it distinguishes between fake products that deceive consumers (primary markets) and those that are openly sold as fakes to consumers (secondary markets – see OECD/EUIPO, 2016). The markets for deceptive and non-deceptive products have significantly different characteristics, and these differences have important implications in the overall assessment.

Secondly, whereas in primary markets consumers pay the full (or approximately) retail price for a fake product thinking it is genuine, consumers knowingly purchasing IPR-infringing products in secondary markets are likely to pay a lower price, and would not necessarily have substituted the fakes for the genuine goods given the choice. Obviously, these differences in price and substitution rates have different implications for estimating lost sales and lost taxes, and for the valuation of consumers' detriment (the price premium unjustly paid by consumers in the belief they are buying a genuine product).

Thirdly, there are other impact areas that are hard to measure quantitatively, or are likely to occur only in the long term; these are therefore excluded from the analysis. They include, for example, the negative effects of counterfeiting and piracy on consumer health and safety, on the environment, on the proliferation of criminal networks, and on long-term innovation and growth.

In sum, there are seven categories of effects that this study quantifies. Four of them are the effects of counterfeit and pirated products smuggled into Italy: 1) loss of consumers' welfare; 2) loss of sales; 3) loss of jobs for the retail and wholesale sector; and 4) lower tax revenues. These four categories are described in detail in Chapter 2.

The three remaining areas are effects caused by global trade in counterfeit and pirated products that infringe Italian IPRs, and are described in Chapter 3. They are: 5) lower sales for IPR owners; 6) job losses for the Italian manufacturing industries; and 7) lower tax revenues.

The methodological framework developed to calculate all these effects, as well as the data used, is presented in detail in the Annex A. Note that it takes account of the "double-counting" issue, which arises from sales of fake products in Italy that infringe the IPRs of its own residents.

Chapter 4 summarises the main findings of the report, and provides suggestions for future research.

References

OHIM (2013), *Impact of intellectual property rights intensive industries in the European Union*, European Union Intellectual Property Office, https://oami.europa.eu/ohimportal/en/web/observatory/ip-contribution (accessed on 5 November 2017).

OECD (2013), *Global Value Chains (GVCs): Italy*, OECD Publishing, Paris, http://www.oecd.org/sti/ind/GVCs%20-%20ITALY.pdf (accessed on 26 February 2018).

OECD/EUIPO (2016), *Trade in Counterfeit and Pirated Goods: Mapping the Economic Impact*, OECD Publishing, Paris, http://dx.doi.org/10.1787/9789264252653-en.

Note

[1] For the purposes of this report the term "counterfeit and pirated" refers to physical goods that infringe trademarks, copyrights, patents or design rights.

2. Counterfeiting in Italy

This chapter profiles the victims, volume, and economic consequences of counterfeit and pirated imports in Italy. It lists the top provenance economies for products seized by Italian customs, and compares the ongoing likelihood of each country to be a source of counterfeit goods sold in Italy. It then describes the product types most likely to be fakes, and – employing new, purpose-built methodology – quantifies the degree of counterfeiting for each. The discussion goes on to distinguish between primary and secondary markets, and explores the factor of "consumer detriment". The chapter concludes with an elaboration of the deleterious effects of counterfeiting for the Italian economy, in terms of consumer welfare, lost sales, lost jobs, and lost government revenue.

2.1. Who is affected and how?

In Italy, imports of counterfeit and pirated products primarily affect:

- Italian retail and wholesale industries
- the Italian government
- Italian consumers.

One could of course argue that Italian IP owners are also negatively affected. That would refer to cases where a fake product smuggled to Italy also infringes Italian IP rights. In order to avoid double counting, those cases are studied in Chapter 3 of this report.

2.1.1. Industry

Legitimate Italian wholesalers and retailers can be badly affected by counterfeit products smuggled into Italy. The damage comes mainly from sales of fake products on secondary markets, i.e. to consumers who knowingly buy them. This in turn leads to lower levels of employment in both sectors.

On the other hand, some industries can actually benefit from counterfeiting. Intermediaries, such as shipping and delivering companies, may record for instance higher demand for their services because of the smuggling of counterfeit goods.

The methodology developed below focuses only on losses incurred by the wholesale and retail industries due to counterfeiting and piracy. It does not take into account either the positive impact of production of counterfeit products, nor potential gains that intermediaries derive from counterfeit trade.

There are two main reasons for this. Firstly, too little is known about the exact nature of counterfeit operations to establish a sound econometric framework that could quantify any potentially positive impact. Secondly, parties that gain from counterfeiting and piracy often operate in an illegal economic environment. The benefits they derive hence do not contribute to social welfare. They instead result in a set of negative externalities, such as erosion of the legal system, corruption of governance structures, and the emergence of criminal networks.

2.1.2. Government

For governments, the principal effects of counterfeit goods smuggling are forgone tax revenues. First of all, the lower sales volume and profits of wholesalers and retailers directly reduce corporate income taxes. Secondly, sales on secondary markets made by wholesalers and retailers are not likely to be registered, which results in reduced sales taxes and value-added taxes. Finally, job losses brought about by counterfeiting reduce payroll taxes, notably social security contributions and personal income taxes.

In the longer term, counterfeit trade can also have broader, more general socio-economic effects on governments, for example relating to trade, innovation and growth, employment, the environment, and criminal activity. However, due to lack of sufficient and consistent cross-economy statistics, quantification of these impacts is not possible at this stage (see Box 2.1).

Box 2.1. The long-term effects of counterfeiting and piracy

The presence of counterfeit and pirated products can have profound long-term implications. For industries, the continued availability of counterfeit products may damage the value of the brand and image of the producers of genuine products. For instance, consumers who purchase fake items in the belief they are genuine will be likely to blame the manufacturer of the genuine product if the fake does not fulfil expectations, thus damaging goodwill. If consumers never discover they have been deceived, they may be reluctant to buy another product from that manufacturer, and may communicate their dissatisfaction to other potential buyers. Also, consumers who purchase the genuine article may be put off by the availability of a counterfeit version. Given that these consumers are aware of potential deception on the primary market, they could adjust their expectations about future consumption.

In addition, lower revenues and profits resulting from counterfeiting and piracy lead in turn to lower investments by rights holders, including investments in research and development (R&D). This could translate into less innovation, slowing technical progress and lowering the rate of economic growth in the longer term.

2.1.3. Consumers

For consumers, counterfeit product smuggling may reduce the value or satisfaction they derive from the products concerned. This is based in large measure on differences from similarly priced products in terms of quality and/or performance. Such differences are likely to be noticed, for instance when a consumer buys a low-quality fake product on the primary market believing it to be a high-quality genuine article.

In addition, counterfeit products dramatically increase the potential for negative effects on the health and safety of consumers. Counterfeiters, who target the primary market, while seeking to maximise profits, have limited or no interest in ensuring the quality, efficacy or safety of their products. However, the regulatory control of supply chain of pharmaceuticals and medical equipment in Italy is efficient. There are no major instances of proliferation of counterfeit pharmaceuticals or medical equipment to the supply chain of genuine goods. In addition, even if such damages occur, they cannot be simply quantified, and so they fall outside the scope of this report.

2.1.4. Overall impact

This study provides an estimate of overall impact of counterfeit product smuggling in four areas:

1. loss of sales for retailers and wholesalers;
2. job losses in the wholesale and retail sector;
3. lower tax revenues; and
4. loss of consumer welfare.

The data and the methodological framework developed to calculate these effects are presented, in Annex A.1 and Annex A.2.

2.2. The market for counterfeit products in Italy

Before calculating the economic consequences of imports of counterfeit and pirated products in Italy, the first step consists in quantifying the volume and the scope of these imports in Italy.

The following paragraphs provide some descriptive statistics on the scope of the market for counterfeit and pirated imports in Italy. Because the value of counterfeit and pirated products seized by customs authorities is likely to represent only a fraction of the actual value of fakes smuggled into the territory, this section uses the General Trade-Related Index of Counterfeiting (GTRIC) methodology developed in OECD/EUIPO (2016) and presented in detail in Annex A.4, to provide a reasonable estimate of the full value.

2.2.1. Where do fake products arriving in Italy mainly come from?

A review of the data on Italian customs seizures shows that counterfeit products imported into Italy between 2011 and 2013 came mainly from China and Hong Kong, China, representing respectively around 50% and 29% of the total value seized by Italian customs (Figure 2.1). They were followed by Greece (6%), Singapore (4%) and Turkey (2%).

Figure 2.1. Top provenance economies for counterfeit products seized by Italian customs, 2011-13

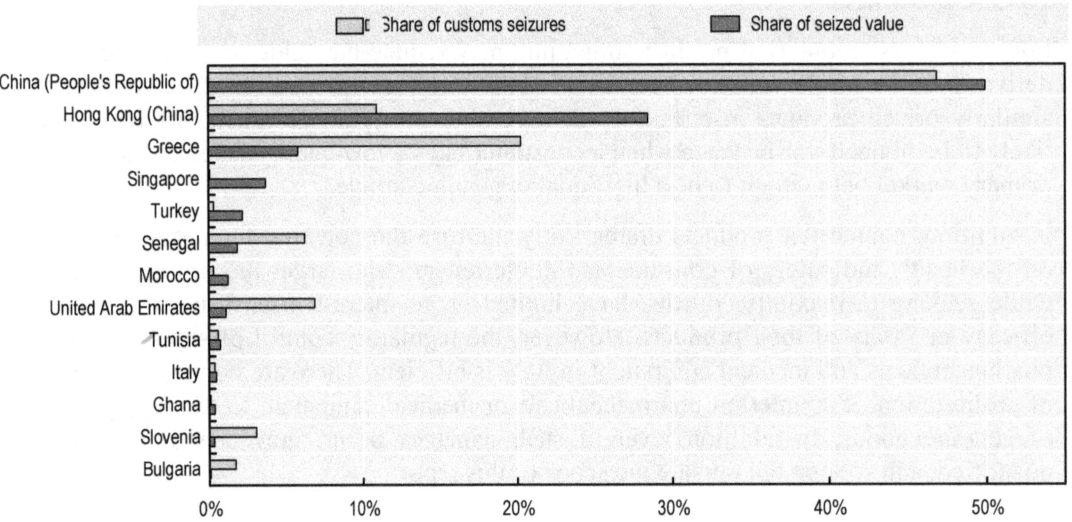

In order to compare the likelihood of each provenance country to be a source of counterfeit goods sold in Italy, these data on customs seizures need to be compared with data on each country's Italian imports and sales of genuine products. This was done using the GTRIC-e index (General Trade-Related Index of Counterfeiting for provenance economies), which compares seizure intensities of counterfeits shipped from a given provenance economy with the share of that provenance economy in Italian imports of genuine goods. GTRIC-e assigns a high score to an economy that is a source of a high value of counterfeit products in absolute terms, or when a large share of Italian imports from that economy is counterfeit.

Table 2.1 shows the top ten economies most likely to be a provenance of counterfeit products smuggled into Italy for the period 2011-2013 (see Table B.1 in Annex B for a complete list). Clearly, some of these provenance economies, led notably by China, appear to be major sources of infringing items

Some of these main provenance economies of counterfeit and pirated products shipped to Italy were identified as key transit points in the global trade of fake goods in the recent OECD/EUIPO (2017) report. These include Hong Kong (China), Singapore, the United Arab Emirates or the Syrian Arab Republic. Other small Asian economies appear as major exporter of fake goods to Italy, but rather as direct producers of these counterfeits. Those include for instance the Philippines, Pakistan, Malaysia, and Thailand. Finally, North African economies, such as Tunisia and Morocco, and Turkey are also identified as key provenance economies of fake goods in Italy. These could be either because they are important producers of counterfeit and pirated goods, or because they are strategic points of transit.

Table 2.1 indicates that a significant share of trade in fake goods with the destination Italy, transits through other EU countries or Balkans, including Greece, Bulgaria, Germany, Slovenia, Albania and Malta. This concurs with interviews conducted with Italian customs, which indicated that many fake goods that eventually end up in Italy, arrive initially to the EU through harbours in western and northern Europe. This fakes are then transported on trucks to Italy, through the extensive and well-developed European networks of highways.

Table 2.1. Economies most likely to be the provenance of counterfeit and pirated imports in Italy

GTRIC-e values, average 2011-2013

Provenance economy	GTRIC-e
China (People's Republic of)	1.000
Hong Kong (China)	1.000
Senegal	1.000
Greece	1.000
United Arab Emirates	0.959
Tunisia	0.864
Bulgaria	0.816
Slovenia	0.774
Morocco	0.762
Turkey	0.726
Singapore	0.663
Philippines	0.568
Pakistan	0.563
Germany	0.462
Peru	0.438
Syrian Arab Republic	0.394
Thailand	0.332
Albania	0.318
Malaysia	0.289
Malta	0.278

Notes: A high GTRIC-e score indicates that an economy is highly prone to be a source of counterfeit products sold in Italy, either in absolute terms or as a share of Italian imports. The results for all provenance economies for years 2011, 2012 and 2013 are reported in Table B.1 in Annex B.

Such intra-EU transiting of counterfeit goods poses numerous challenges for Italian customs. According to the EU regulations goods are cleared upon arrival to the EU, even if their final destination is in another member state. However, customs officers at arrival ports other than Italy might perceive smuggling of counterfeit goods destined to another member state as a risk of relatively lower priority. In addition customs controls by Italian customs of goods that enter Italy from other EU member states by road would be extremely costly and difficult, and clearly would pose a big obstacle for trade overall.

Consequently, the risk of interception of counterfeits destined for Italy seems to be lower if counterfeiters decide to enter the EU through Member States other than Italy.

During several structured interviews, Italian customs confirmed this phenomenon. Random checks of transportation from other EU member countries performed sporadically at the Mt. Blanc tunnel connecting Italy and France, revealed a large volume of counterfeit goods aiming at Italy, which originated outside the EU.

Similarly alarming trends are observed in the context of small postal and express service shipments. According to interviews carried out the Italian enforcement authorities, the volume of counterfeits shipped through small consignments keeps growing. In addition the majority of fakes shipped via small parcels come from other EU countries, most of which arrived via the biggest airport hubs for small parcels, such as Leipzig (Germany), East Midlands (UK) and Liege (Belgium).[1]

The last interesting trend is the large number of seized IP-infringing packaging and labelling material being smuggled into Italy (Box 2.2).

Box 2.2. IP-infringing labels and packaging materials

An analysis of the seizures database, and interviews with the Italian enforcement officials confirm the large number of seized IP-infringing packaging and labels being smuggled to Italy.

The packaging, labels and logos are sent separately from the products to be counterfeited; oftentimes these products are sent without any trademarks. Since these 'no name' goods do not infringe any trademark (just design rights in some cases) they are much more difficult to be spotted and seized by enforcement authorities. The final labelling takes place at a later stage somewhere in Italy or in other EU member states.

This approach greatly reduces the risk to counterfeiters of interception and detention; in these cases interception is limited mostly to the seizure of, packaging, and the like. This changing strategy of counterfeiters confirms findings formulated in a study by OHIM and Europol (2015) about the domestic assembly of counterfeit and pirated products from imported materials.

2.2.2. Which product types are most likely to be counterfeited?

The dataset on customs seizures of IP-infringing goods smuggled into Italy can also be used to quantify infringed product types in that country. It should be noted that in 2013, a wide range of product categories were subject to counterfeiting in Italy (see Figure 2.2). This means that any type of product for which IP adds economic value, and thus creates price differentials, will become a target for counterfeiters and a potential threat to the Italian economy and society.

While a broad range of goods are sensitive to infringement, the intensity of counterfeiting varies significantly across product categories. This is supported by seizures statistics shown in Figure 2.2, which are concentrated in a relatively limited number of product categories, including articles of leather and handbags; ICT devices; clothing; watches; jewellery and sunglasses.

Figure 2.2. Share of seizures of counterfeit goods in Italy by product type, 2011-13

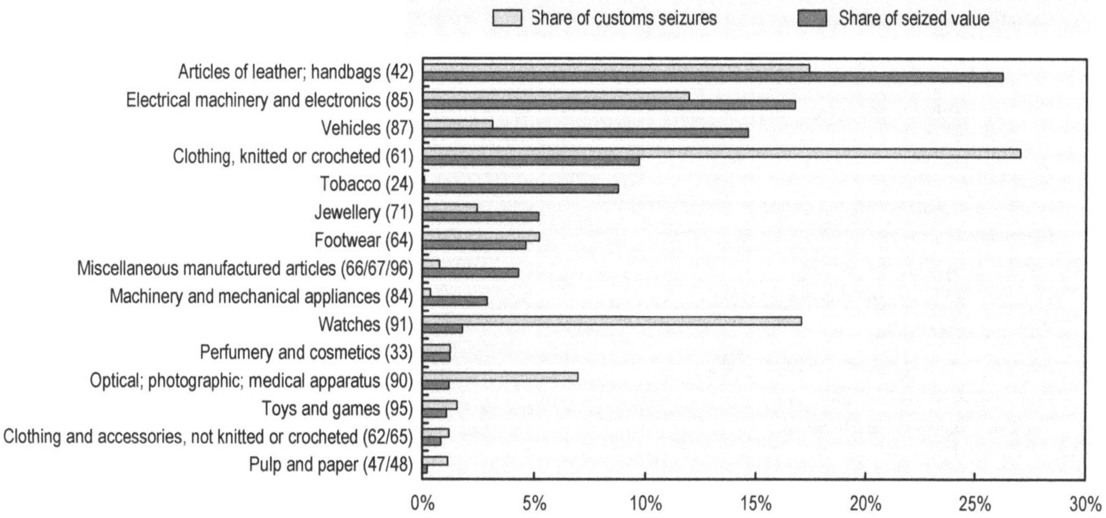

Note: Figures in parenthesis are Harmonized System (HS) codes as defined by the United Nations Trade Statistics (UN Trade Statistics, 2017).

A meaningful measure of the likelihood of different types of infringing products to be sold in Italy can be obtained using the GTRIC-p index (General Trade-Related Index of Counterfeiting for product categories). As with GTRIC-e, the seizure intensity of a given product category is compared with the share of this product category in Italian imports of genuine goods. The result is a ranking of products smuggled into Italy by the likelihood that they will be counterfeit (see Table B.2 in Appendix B for the complete list).

Table 2.2. Top 25 product categories in terms of likelihood of being counterfeited

GTRIC-p scores, average 2011-2013

Product category (HS codes)	GTRIC-p
Watches (91)	1.000
Articles of leather; handbags (42)	1.000
Clothing, knitted or crocheted (61)	1.000
Tobacco (24)	0.999
Miscellaneous manufactured articles (66/67/96)	0.999
Toys and games (95)	0.985
Footwear (64)	0.965
Perfumery and cosmetics (33)	0.904
Printed articles (49)	0.866
Optical; photographic; medical apparatus (90)	0.857
Electrical machinery and electronics (85)	0.831
Vehicles (87)	0.513
Jewellery (71)	0.483
Clothing and accessories, not knitted or crocheted (62/65)	0.436
Plastic and articles thereof (39)	0.374
Tanning or dyeing extracts (32)	0.368
Machinery and mechanical appliances (84)	0.353
Pulp and paper (47/48)	0.330
Iron and steel; and articles thereof (72/73)	0.296
Pharmaceutical products (30)	0.264
Tools and cutlery of base metal (82)	0.239
Foodstuffs (02-21)	0.222
Rubber and article thereof (40)	0.213
Glass and glassware (70)	0.181
Furniture (94)	0.178

Notes: A high GTRIC-p score signals a product category that is more likely to be counterfeit – that is to say, it contains high euro values for counterfeit products, or a large share of Italian sales in that product category is counterfeit. Figures in parenthesis are Harmonized System (HS) codes as defined by the United Nations Trade Statistics (UN Trade Statistics, 2017). Values are zero for HS categories non-displayed in this table.

2.2.3. What is the total value of counterfeit products sold in Italy?

The best estimates – based on the data provided by customs authorities and on the GTRIC methodology – indicate that imports of counterfeit and pirated products in Italy accounted for as much as EUR 10.4 billion in 2013, the equivalent of 3% of Italian imports of genuine goods. The term "as much as" is crucial here, as it refers to the upper limit of counterfeit and pirated products imported in Italy. In addition, this amount does not include domestically produced and consumed counterfeit and pirated products and pirated digital products that are distributed via the internet.

The analysis also reveals that the degree of counterfeiting in Italy varies considerably across product categories. In terms of sectors with the highest share of fakes in imports, articles of leather and handbags were on top. 15.3% of goods imported to Italy in this category were fakes. It was followed by toys and games with 14.3% (see Table 2.3 for the top 18 categories in 2013; and Table B.3 in Annex B for complete results by HS categories for years 2011, 2012, 2013).

Table 2.3. Top product categories subject to counterfeiting in Italian imports in relative terms, 2013

In terms of share within the product category

HS category	Share of fake imports
Articles of leather; handbags (42)	15.3%
Toys and games (95)	14.3%
Miscellaneous manufactured articles (66/67/96); *incl. luxury pens, cuff-links, pins, lighters and umbrellas.*	13.4%
Clothing, knitted or crocheted (61)	12.7%
Footwear (64)	10.8%
Watches (91)	9.8%
Printed articles (49); *including fake packaging and boxes made for domestic assembly.*	9.6%
Electrical machinery and electronics (85); *incl. a wide range of ICT devices.*	9.3%
Optical; photographic; medical apparatus (90); *incl. sunglasses*	9.0%
Tobacco (24)	7.7%
Perfumery and cosmetics (33)	5.8%
Clothing and accessories, not knitted or crocheted (62/65)	5.8%
Vehicles (87); incl. spare parts and car accessories	4.2%
Jewellery (71)	3.6%
Machinery and mechanical appliances (84); *incl. computers, tablets, machine tools, household appliances.*	3.5%
Tanning or dyeing extracts (32); *incl. toner cartridges.*	3.5%
Plastic and articles thereof (39); *including fake plastic packaging made for domestic assembly.*	3.1%
Tools and cutlery of base metal (82); *incl. hand tools; buttons; razor blade.*	2.4%
Other made-up textile articles (63); *incl. carpets; blankets; pillows.*	2.2%

Note: Figures in parenthesis are Harmonized System (HS) codes as defined by the United Nations Trade Statistics (UN Trade Statistics, 2017[17]).

In absolute terms, ICT devices (electrical and electronic components) were the most counterfeited type of goods, with an estimated value of EUR 2.3 billion of fakes imported in Italy. This category includes a wide range of devices, such as mobile phones, DVD players, headphones, earphones, microphones, batteries etc. It was followed by fake machinery and mechanical appliances (e.g. computers, tablets, household appliances, vacuum cleaners) with fake imports equal to around EUR 1 billion (see Table 2.4 for the top categories); and Table B.3 in Annex B for complete results by HS categories for years 2011, 2012, 2013).

It should be highlighted that these findings are in line with other relevant research and statistics. The overall shift of counterfeit products from top-end consumer goods to virtually all product categories for which IP offers profit margin has been observed in other markets. A relevant example is the ICT industry that recently has been particularly targeted. This has been confirmed by numerous publications by the OECD (2017), EUIPO-ITU (2017), or by the EC JRC and Politecnico di Milano (Thumm et. al, 2018).

Table 2.4. Top product categories subject to counterfeiting in Italian imports in absolute terms, 2013

HS Category	Vaule in EUR mn
Electrical machinery and electronics (85); incl. a wide range of ICT.	2263
Machinery and mechanical appliances (84); incl. computers, tablets, machine tools.	1076
Vehicles (87); incl. spare parts and car accessories.	1023
Optical; photographic; medical apparatus (90); incl. sunglasses.	781
Clothing, knitted or crocheted (61)	725
Footwear (64)	495
Foodstuffs (02-21)	481
Plastic and articles thereof (39); including fake plastic packaging made for domestic assembly.	476
Iron and steel; and articles thereof (72/73); incl. kitchen tools; cookware; keys; sanitary ware; gas stoves.	392
Articles of leather; handbags (42)	352
Clothing and accessories, not knitted or crocheted (62/65)	328
Pharmaceutical products (30); incl. lifestyle drugs.	297
Jewellery (71)	283
Toys and games (95)	247
Tobacco (24)	158
Perfumery and cosmetics (33)	134
Watches (91)	128
Miscellaneous manufactured articles (66/67/96); incl. luxury pens, cuff-links, pins, lighters and umbrellas.	126

Note: Figures in parenthesis are Harmonized System (HS) codes as defined by the United Nations Trade Statistics (UN Trade Statistics, 2017).

2.3. The primary and secondary markets for counterfeit products sold in Italy

Two questions are crucial in assessing the economic impact of counterfeit products smuggled into Italy for domestic retail and wholesale industries, consumers, and the government. First, what is the proportion of counterfeit products that are sold on primary versus secondary markets in Italy? Second, within secondary markets, what is the rate at which Italian consumers are substituting counterfeit goods for legitimate products?

The distinction between primary and secondary markets described earlier is a critical one. Every sale of a fake item on a primary market clearly represents a direct loss for the retail and wholesale industry. In secondary markets, however, only a share of consumers would have deliberately substituted their purchases of counterfeit products for legitimate ones. This is because in secondary markets consumers know what they are buying is fake, and they decide to proceed with the purchase for a number of possible reasons (see Box 2.3). The key issue then is how to calculate the consumers' substitution rate, i.e. the extent to which every illegal purchase displaces a legal sale.

Box 2.3. Why do people buy fakes knowingly?

There are numerous reasons identified in the scientific literature for why people buy fakes. Firstly, if the genuine product is hard to get hold of, this might greatly increase the perception of its value. Furthermore, the willingness of consumers to purchase a counterfeit product seems to increase if they can rate its quality before purchase and to decrease if they cannot. The situation surrounding the purchase also determines purchase intentions. The situational mood explains why some people are more prone to buy counterfeits even if that is illegal or they experience post-purchase dissatisfaction with a product of low quality. Recent psychological research illustrates a number of other motivations, such as the "thrill of the hunt" for what's fake being part of a "secret society", and genuine interest. Buyers of counterfeit products also try to legitimise and justify their behaviour.

Sources: Bian, Haque and Smith (2015); Bian et al. (2016); Eisend and Schuchert-Güler (2006)

The methodology used to calculate the share of primary and secondary markets in Italy is presented in Step 2 of Annex A.2, while Table 2.4 below identifies the secondary and, consequently, primary markets for counterfeit products sold in Italy by sector. This shows that 51.1% of imported counterfeit and pirated products sold in Italy in 2013 were sold to consumers who actually knew they were buying fake products, with the remaining share purchased unwittingly. The share of fakes destined for secondary markets varies significantly by sector, ranging from 15% for foodstuff to 60% for watches and jewellery and ICT devices.

Table 2.5. Share of secondary markets for counterfeit products in Italy, 2013

Sector	Share secondary markets
Food, beverages and tobacco	15.35%
Chemical and allied products; except pharmaceuticals, perfumery and cosmetics	23.33%
Pharmaceutical and medicinal chemical products	28.57%
Perfumery and cosmetics	62.61%
Textiles and other intermediate products (e.g. plastics; rubbers; paper; wood)	46.10%
Clothing, footwear, leather and related products	50.02%
Watches and jewellery	58.35%
Non-metallic mineral products (e.g. glass and glass products, ceramic products)	30.00%
Basic metals and fabricated metal products (except machinery and equipment)	17.14%
Electronic and electrical equipment, optical products, scientific instruments	60.03%
Machinery, industrial equipment; computers and peripheral equipment; ships and aircrafts	36.94%
Motor vehicles and motorcycles	55.29%
Household cultural and recreation goods; including toys and games, books and musical instruments	43.26%
Furniture, lighting equipment, carpets and other manufacturing n.e.c	37.59%
Total	51.12%

Once the shares of primary and secondary markets are identified, the next key question is how to calculate the consumers' substitution rate on secondary markets – i.e. the extent to which every illegal purchase displaces a legal sale. Information on substitution rates can be obtained from two different sources: academic research on consumers' socio-economic behaviour, and consumer surveys. The majority of academic research has focused on intangible pirated products, such as digital piracy; findings are rarer for tangible products, with the exception of luxury items.

There are several studies that report estimates on consumers' substitutions rates. The first one is the Anti-Counterfeiting Group's (2007) consumer survey that looked at various product categories (Anti-Counterfeiting Group, 2007). It determined a 39% substitution rate for clothing and footwear, meaning that every EUR 2.5 spent on fake clothes, accessories or footwear in secondary markets translates into EUR 1 in lost sales for the retail and wholesale industry. The same survey determined the 49% substitution rate for products related to the perfumery and cosmetics sector, and 27% for products belonging to the watch and jewellery industries. Another study on substitution rates was a survey by (Tom et al., 1998) that determined the rate of 32% for all other fake products sold on secondary markets.

Table 2.6 summarises the substitution rates used in this study.

Table 2.6. Assumed consumer substitution rates in the main scenario

Sector	Substitution rate
Perfumery and cosmetics	49%
Watches and jewellery	27%
Clothing, accessories, leather and related products	39%
Other sectors	32%

Sources: Anti-Counterfeiting Group (2007) and Tom et al. (1998).

The general shortage of data on substitution rates between fake and genuine goods is in fact the main challenge in the overall quantitative exercise on the effects of counterfeiting. Therefore, such exercise includes a sensitivity analysis that checks if changes in substitution rates could significantly bias final results. The analysis is done by introducing three different scenarios, with three different sets of substitution rates (see Box 2.4). The results of the sensitivity analysis are summarised in the Annex A.6.

Importantly, the estimated results for the three scenarios as presented in the Annex A.6 are very close to each other. This re-confirms the robustness of all the results presented in the analysis.

Box 2.4. Sensitivity analysis of substitution rates

The sensitivity analysis is done to address the scarcity of data on substitution rates between fake and genuine goods. To do it, three different scenarios are introduced.

The first assumes substitution rates that follow the results of the Anti-Counterfeiting Group's (2007) consumer survey. In this scenario, a substitution rate of 39% has been chosen for the product category related to clothing and footwear, meaning that every EUR 2.5 spent on fake clothes, accessories or footwear in secondary markets translates into EUR 1 in lost sales for the retail and wholesale industry. Also in accordance with this consumer survey, the selected rates in scenario 1 are 49% for products related to the perfumery and cosmetics sector, and 27% for products belonging to the watch and jewellery industries. Finally, according to the study carried out by Tom et al. (1998), the selected substitution rate is 32% for all other fake products sold on secondary markets.

The second scenario is more conservative, and assumes substitution rates 10 percentage points lower. The third scenario is the most conservative one, and assumes the substitution rates to be 20 percentage points lower than in the first scenario.

In order to test the robustness of the results, they are calculated based on these three alternative scenarios, all based on lower assumed consumer substitution rates. The three are recapped in the Table 2.7 below.

Table 2.7. Assumed consumer substitution rates in the three performed scenarios

Sector	Scenario 1	Scenario 2	Scenario 3
Perfumery and cosmetics	49%	39%	29%
Watches and jewellery	27%	17%	7%
Clothing, accessories, leather and related products	39%	29%	19%
Other sectors	32%	22%	12%

Sources: Author's own calculations based on Anti-Counterfeiting Group (2007) and Tom et al. (1998).

2.4. To what extent are Italian consumers overpaying for fake products?

While consumers who knowingly purchase fake products are prepared to accept any trade-off between cost and quality, consumers who unwittingly purchase fake goods end up paying an excessive price for a low-quality product. As explained in Step 3 in Annex A.2, this "consumer detriment" can be estimated by the average price premium earned by counterfeiters from both markets, times the volume of fake goods sold on primary markets.

The estimates for consumer detriment in Italy were thus calculated in two steps. The first was to calculate for each sector the difference between average prices on primary and secondary markets. These differences represent the individual consumer detriment from an individual purchase. Second, this individual detriment was multiplied by the total volume of transactions on the primary market in a product category.

The estimates for consumer detriment in Italy are presented in Table 2.8. In 2013, the highest detriment was recorded for watches and jewellery (EUR 1.42 billion). The total detriment due to consumer deception in 2013 amounted to almost EUR 2 billion.

Table 2.8. Estimate of consumer detriment in Italy by sector, 2013

Sector	Value in EUR mn
Food, beverages and tobacco	53.9
Chemical and allied products; except pharmaceuticals, perfumery and cosmetics	0.6
Pharmaceutical and medicinal chemical products	5.3
Perfumery and cosmetics	15.0
Textiles and other intermediate products (e.g. plastics; rubbers; paper; wood)	1.3
Clothing, footwear, leather and related products	253.0
Watches and jewellery	1420.0
Basic metals and fabricated metal products (except machinery and equipment)	0.8
Electronic and electrical equipment, optical products, scientific instruments	66.5
Machinery, industrial equipment; computers and peripheral equipment; ships and aircrafts	8.2
Motor vehicles and motorcycles	19.3
Household cultural and recreation goods; including toys and games, books and musical instruments	64.9
Furniture, lighting equipment, carpets and other manufacturing n.e.c	1.8
Total	1910.6

2.5. The effect of fake goods on sales in the Italian retail and wholesale sector

The sales lost due to the counterfeiting market in the Italian retail and wholesale sector are calculated using the methodology presented in Step 4 of Annex A.2. It is done using the substitution rates determined in the existing literature: 39% for the product category relating to clothing and footwear; 49% for products relating to the perfumery and cosmetics sector; 27% for products belonging to the watch and jewellery industries; and 32% for all other fake products sold on secondary markets.

Overall, the total volume of forgone sales in the Italian wholesale and retail sector due to counterfeit and pirated imports in 2013 was EUR 6.9 billion. This is equivalent to 2.7% of total sales in that Italian wholesale and retail sector the same year.

The highest sale losses to the Italian wholesale and retail industries in absolute terms were for electronic, electrical and optical products (EUR 1.8 billion in forgone sales in 2013), followed by clothing, footwear, leather and related products (EUR 1.3 billion in forgone sales in 2013).

The sector of "watches and jewellery" experienced the highest losses in relative terms (7.5% of forgone sales due to the counterfeiting market). It was followed by the sector of electronic, electrical and optical products (5.4%) and that of clothing, footwear, leather and related products (4.4%).

Table 2.9. Lost sales for the Italian retail and wholesale sector due to fake imports in Italy, 2013

Sector	Value in EUR mn	Share of sales
Food, beverages and tobacco	618	1.0%
Chemical and allied products; except pharmaceuticals, perfumery and cosmetics	125	3.7%
Pharmaceutical and medicinal chemical products	254	2.3%
Perfumery and cosmetics	85	1.6%
Textiles and other intermediate products (e.g. plastics; rubbers; paper; wood)	446	4.3%
Clothing, footwear, leather and related products	1269	4.4%
Watches and jewellery	221	7.5%
Non-metallic mineral products (e.g. glass and glass products, ceramic products)	16	0.2%
Basic metals and fabricated metal products (except machinery and equipment)	475	4.0%
Electronic and electrical equipment, optical products, scientific instruments	1794	5.4%
Machinery, industrial equipment; computers and peripheral equipment	732	4.1%
Motor vehicles and motorcycles	569	1.9%
Household cultural and recreation goods; including toys and games, and musical instruments	212	2.1%
Furniture, lighting equipment, carpets and other manufacturing n.e.c	132	0.6%
Total wholesale and resale sector	6949	2.7%

2.6. The effect of the counterfeiting market on jobs in the Italian retail and wholesale industry

Lower sales in the retail and wholesale industries reduce the demand for labour, and consequently lead to job losses. However, a $x\%$ decrease in sales does not necessarily translate into a corresponding decrease of $x\%$ in jobs, such that the extent to which each wholesale and retail industry adjusts employment when sales vary first needs to be calculated. The basic econometric model presented in Step 5 in Annex A.2 makes it possible to estimate these industry-specific elasticities. Combining these industry-specific elasticities of employment with the estimated lost sales detailed in the previous section allows then estimating the number and share of lost jobs within wholesale and retail industries.

Table 2.10 presents the main results for various branches of the wholesale and retail sector. Total job losses in the Italian retail and wholesale sector due to counterfeiting imports in Italy amounted to more than 23,150 in 2013, equivalent to more than 1.3% of all people employed in the sector.

In absolute terms, the highest job losses due to counterfeiting and piracy were found in the sales of clothing, footwear, accessories and related products: 6582, or 2.4% of all employees in the sectors listed. In relative terms, the wholesalers and retails in the watches and jewellery sector were the most affected, incurring 3.6% of job losses in 2013.

Table 2.10. Lost jobs in the Italian retail and wholesale sector due to fake imports in Italy, 2013

Sector	Number of employees	Share of employees
Food, beverages and tobacco	3374	0.6%
Chemical and allied products; except pharmaceuticals, perfumery and cosmetics	244	1.7%
Pharmaceutical and medicinal chemical products	565	1.2%
Perfumery and cosmetics	340	0.9%
Textiles and other intermediate products (e.g. plastics; rubbers; paper; wood)	1847	2.3%
Clothing, footwear, leather and related products	6582	2.4%
Watches and jewellery	797	3.6%
Non-metallic mineral products (e.g. glass and glass products, ceramic products)	65	0.1%
Basic metals and fabricated metal products (except machinery and equipment)	1649	2.1%
Electronic and electrical equipment, optical products, scientific instruments	1712	2.7%
Machinery, industrial equipment; computers and peripheral equipment	2262	2.1%
Motor vehicles and motorcycles	2272	1.1%
Household cultural and recreation goods; including toys and games and musical instruments	813	1.1%
Furniture, lighting equipment, carpets and other manufacturing n.e.c	629	0.3%
Total wholesale and retail sector	23149	1.3%

Note: Employees are measured in full time equivalent units according to Eurostat (2018)[2] definition.

2.7. Losses in government revenues due to sales of fake goods

Lower sales in the wholesale and retail sector due to counterfeit and pirated imports in Italy mean lower tax revenues for the Italian Government from value-added tax (VAT), corporate income tax (CIT), personal income tax (PIT) and social security contributions (see Step 6 in Annex A.2).

Table 2.11 presents this forgone revenue by type of taxes, which amounted to EUR 3.7 billion in 2013. Within this overall figure, the largest component was forgone value added taxes, amounting to EUR 1.5 billion.

Table 2.11. Forgone taxes for the Italian government due fake imports in Italy, 2013

Tax type	Value in EUR mn	Share of collected taxes
Personal income taxes and social security contributions	1354	0.8%
Corporate income taxes	831	2.1%
Value added taxes	1529	1.6%
Total	3714	1.2%

Finally, one should keep in mind that the degree of tax loss also depends on the efficiency of tax collection schemes. An inefficient fiscal system might allow companies to exploit gaps and mismatches in tax rules to artificially shift profits to low- or no-tax locations where there is little or no economic activity. The OECD Base Erosion and Profit Shifting programme (BEPS) was designed to tackle this problem (Box 2.5). According to its recent findings based on country-by-country reporting, Italy is one of the countries with the most advanced legislative framework to counter this problem.

Box 2.5. The OECD BEPS programme

The OECD Base Erosion and Profit Shifting (BEPS) programme tackles tax avoidance strategies that exploit gaps and mismatches in tax rules to artificially shift profits to low- or no-tax locations. Although some of the schemes used are illegal, most are not. However, the practice undermines the fairness and integrity of tax systems because businesses that operate across borders can use BEPS to gain a competitive advantage over enterprises that operate at a domestic level. Moreover, when taxpayers see multinational corporations legally avoiding income tax, it undermines voluntary compliance by all taxpayers.

Under the BEPS framework, over 100 economies collaborate to implement measures to counter these strategies. The Inclusive Framework presents information on the domestic legal frameworks based on country-by-country (CbC) reporting around the world; in so doing, it has provided tax administrations with a high-level snapshot of the measures currently being implemented.

References

Anti-Counterfeiting Group (2007), *Consumer survey*, commisioned from independent survey specialists, http://www.wipo.int/ip-outreach/en/tools/research/details.jsp?id=691.

Bian, X., S. Haque and A. Smith (2015), "Social power, product conspicuousness and the demand for luxury brand counterfeit products", *British Journal of Social Psychology*, Vol. 54/1, pp. 37-54.

Bian et al. (2016), "New insights into unethical counterfeit consumption", *Journal of Business Research*, Vol. 69/10, pp. 4249-58.

Brembo (2015), *New Anti-Counterfeiting Car Will Protect Buyers of Brembo High Perforance and Racing Products*, Brembo S.p.A, Curno (Bergamo), http://www.brembo.com/en/company/news/brembo-puts-the-brakes-on-counterfeit-products (accessed on 26 February 2018).

Censis (2016), *La contraffazione : dimensioni, caratteristiche e approfondimenti*, Centro Studi Investimenti Sociali, commissioned e funded by the Direzione Generale per la lotta alla contraffazione – UIBM, Ministero dello Sviluppo Economico, Rome, http://www.uibm.gov.it/attachments/REPORT%20CENSIS%20FINALE.PDF

Eisend, M. and P. Schuchert-Güler (2006), "Explaining counterfeit purchases: A review and preview", *Academy of Marketing Science Review*, Vol. 2006/12, pp. 1-25.

OECD (2017), *Trade in Counterfeit ICT Goods*, OECD Publishing, Paris, http://oe.cd/fakeICTs.

Eurostat (2018), Structural Business Statistics, Statistical office of the European Union, Luxembourg, http://ec.europa.eu/eurostat/cache/metadata/fr/sbs_esms.htm (last accessed on May 2018)

OECD/EUIPO (2016), *Trade in Counterfeit and Pirated Goods: Mapping the Economic*

Impact, OECD Publishing, Paris, http://dx.doi.org/10.1787/9789264252653-en.

OHIM / Europol (2015), 2015 Situation Report on Counterfeiting in the European Union, Available at: https://www.europol.europa.eu/publications-documents/2015-situation-report-counterfeiting-in-european-union

Thumm, N., Butticé, V. Caviggioli, F., Franzoni, C. and G. Scellato (2018), "Impact of counterfeiting on the performance of digital technology companies", JRC Working Papers on Digital Economy, No 2018-03, EU Joint Research Center, Seville

Tom, G. et al. (1998), "Consumer demand for counterfeit goods", *Psychology & Marketing*, Vol. 15/5, pp. 405-421.

UN Trade Statistics (2017), *Harmonized commodity description and coding systems (HS)*, United Nations, Geneva, https://unstats.un.org/unsd/tradekb/Knowledgebase/50018/Harmonized-Commodity-Description-and-Coding-Systems-HS.

Notes

[1] The Italian enforcement authorities noted that a large share of small parcels arriving by air to Italy from outside the EU is also not destined to Italy. The arrival airports in Italy for small parcels are: Bergamo, Bologna, Milan Linate, Milan Malpensa, Pisa, Rome Fiumicino, Rome Ciampino and Venezia.

[2] Eurostat (2018) defines employees as those persons who work for an employer and who have a contract of employment and receive compensation in the form of wages, salaries, fees, gratuities, piecework pay or remuneration in kind. A worker from an employment agency is considered to be an employee of that temporary employment agency and not of the unit (customer) in which they work.

3. Made in Italy? Infringement of Italian IPRs world wide

This chapter appraises the damage caused by infringement of Italian intellectual property rights in world trade. Having described who suffers in particular from this illicit activity, the discussion goes on to consider the scope and volume of such infringements. The top destination and provenance economies for counterfeit goods that infringe Italian IPR are enumerated. The focus then shifts to the Italian products that are most susceptible to counterfeiting, with a unique quantitative analysis establishing their actual degree of susceptibility. Distinctions are made between primary and secondary markets. Finally, stock is taken of the detrimental effects of IPR infringement on the Italian economy – once again, in terms of lost sales, lost jobs, and lost government revenue.

3.1. Who is affected and how?

Infringement of Italian intellectual property rights (IPRs) in world trade mainly affects:

- Italian right holders (manufacturing industries), and
- the Italian government.

3.1.1. Industry

Legitimate Italian IPR holders can be badly affected by world trade in counterfeit products that infringe their rights. In the short term, such trade reduces sales volumes and hence lowers profits, in turn leading to lower levels of employment in the Italian manufacturing sector. In the long term, Italian companies face significant brand erosion because of unfair competition from counterfeiters that freeride on their IP.

The methodology developed below focuses only on the short-run economic effects on sales volumes and manufacturing employment. The long-term effects cannot be quantified, for two main reasons. First, to do so would generally require data spanning several years, and such data are unavailable. Secondly, existing studies that could help produce an adequate alternative methodology are mostly theoretical and do not provide robust empirical support.

It is also important to note that, as mentioned in the previous chapter, some industries can actually benefit from counterfeiting and piracy. Firstly, counterfeiting can generate economic activity, which can be beneficial for many industry players if the fake goods are produced domestically. Secondly, some intermediaries, such as express and shipping companies, may record higher demand for their services because of counterfeit trade.

This methodology however focuses only on losses incurred by the manufacturing industry due to counterfeiting and piracy, and does not take into account either the positive impact of production of counterfeit products, or potential gains that intermediaries derive from counterfeit trade. The two main reasons for this have been advanced in Section 2.1 of Chapter Two.

3.1.2. Government

For the Italian government, the principal effects of the global trade in counterfeit and pirated products that infringe Italian trademarks and patents are forgone tax revenues. Firstly, lower sales volume and profits made by Italian rights holders directly reduce corporate income taxes. Secondly, some sales of these products made on the domestic market are not likely to be registered, which results in reduced sales and value-added taxes. Finally, manufacturing job losses brought about by counterfeiting reduce payroll taxes, notably social security contributions and personal income taxes.

As presented in Chapter Two, in the longer term, counterfeit trade can also have some broader, more general damaging effects for governments, such as those on trade, innovation and growth, employment, the environment, and criminal activity. However, due to lack of sufficient and consistent cross-economy statistics, quantification of these impacts is not possible at this stage.

To summarise, there are three impact areas of world trade in products that infringe Italian trademarks and patents this study is able to quantify with a relatively high degree of robustness: 1) lower sales, 2) job losses for the Italian manufacturing industry, and 3) lower tax revenues for the Italian Government.

The data and the methodological framework developed to calculate all these effects are presented step by step in Annex A.3. The following subsections present the methodology and its main results.

3.2. What are the scope and volume of Italian IP infringements in global trade?

Before calculating the impacts of Italian IP infringements in global trade on the Italian economy, the first step is to evaluate the volume of such infringements. The following paragraphs thus provide some descriptive statistics on the global scope of trade in counterfeit products that infringe Italian trademarks and patents. It then uses the GTRIC methodology presented in details in Step 7 in Annex A.3 and Annex A.5 to estimate the total volume of infringing counterfeit and pirated products traded worldwide.

3.2.1. What are the top destination and provenance economies for counterfeit goods that infringe Italian IPR?

Interestingly, a review of the data on global customs seizures highlights that the member countries of the European Union were the top destinations for counterfeit and pirated products that infringed Italian IPR between 2011 and 2013 (Figure 3.1.B), in terms of both the number of customs seizures and seized value. Italy itself ranked fourth in terms of the seized value of these products, and second in terms of the number of customs seizures.

Asian economies, particularly China, Hong Kong, China and Thailand, were the main provenance of counterfeit and pirated goods that infringed Italian IPR over the same period 2011-13 (see Figure 3.1.A), followed by Turkey, Greece and Morocco.

In order to obtain a meaningful measure of the likelihood of each economy becoming a destination for counterfeit and pirated products whose IP rights are held by Italian residents, these data on customs seizures need to be compared with data on Italian exports of genuine products and data on Italian manufacturing domestic sales. Use is therefore made of the GTRIC-e index (General Trade-Related Index for destination economies), which allows comparison of the customs seizure frequency of counterfeit products that infringed Italian IPR and are sold in a given economy, and the share of this economy in Italian sales (exports plus domestic sales).

Table 3.1 lists the top 15 economies most likely to be destinations for counterfeit and pirated products infringing IPR of Italian holders over the period 2011-13 (see Table B.3 in Annex B for a complete list). The range of likely destination economies is very large, ranging from Paraguay, Kuwait, EU (e.g. Spain, Portugal, the United Kingdom, Finland, the Netherlands) to south-eastern European economies (the Former Yugoslav Republic of Macedonia, Montenegro).

Figure 3.1. Top provenance and destination economies of fake goods infringing Italian IP, 2011-13

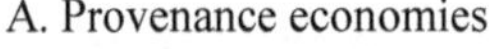

A. Provenance economies

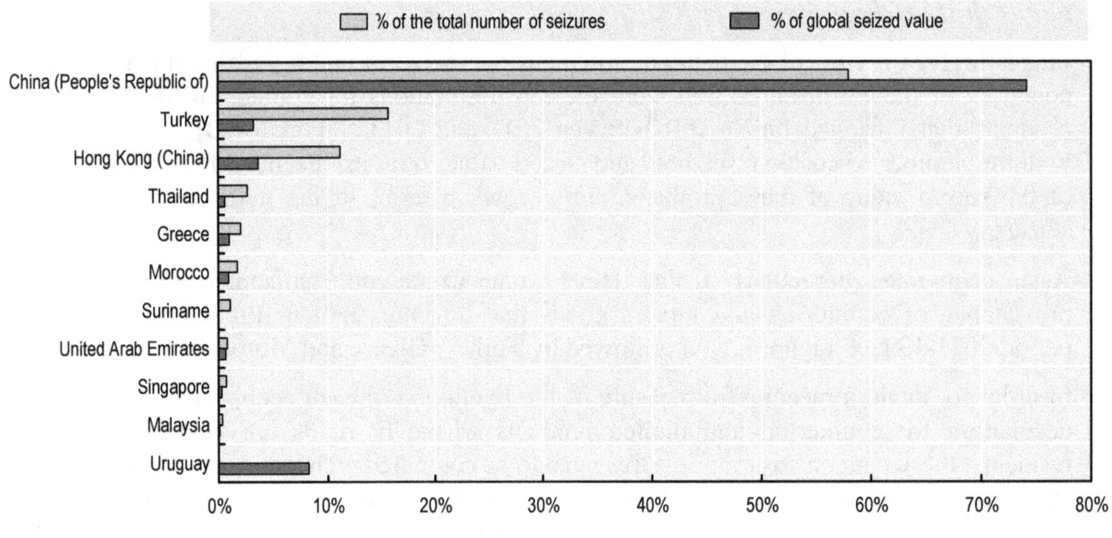

B. Destination economies

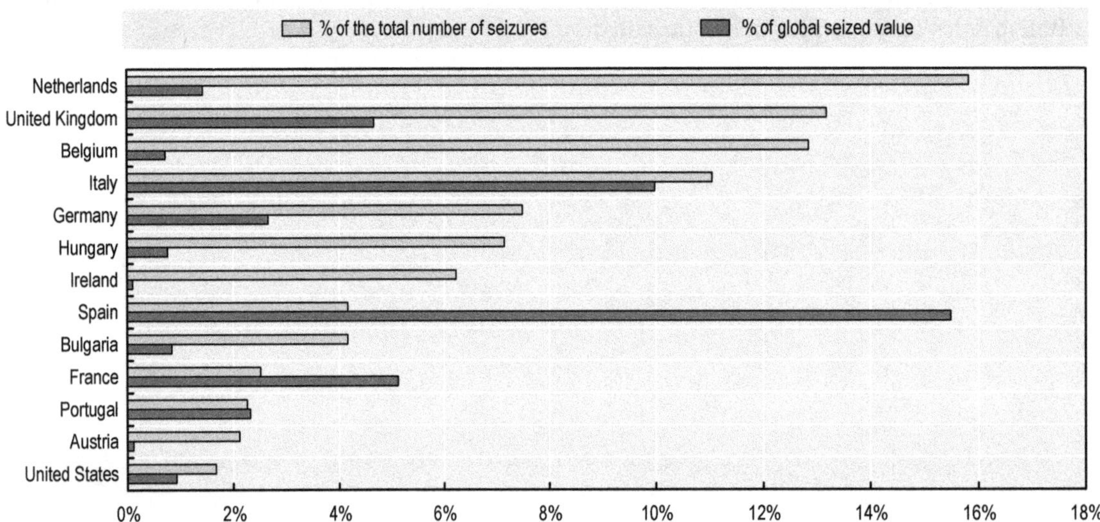

Table 3.1. Top 15 economies most likely to import products infringing Italian IPR

GTRIC-e scores, average 2011-2013

Destination economy	GTRIC-e
Paraguay	1.000
Kuwait	0.983
Czech Republic	0.975
Spain	0.974
Bulgaria	0.952
Portugal	0.945
Togo	0.924
Luxembourg	0.920
Guinea	0.881
United Kingdom	0.871
Former Yugoslav Republic of Macedonia	0.784
Finland	0.778
Hungary	0.768
Netherlands	0.767
Montenegro	0.750

Notes: A high GTRIC-e score indicates that an economy is highly prone to be a destination market for counterfeit products infringing Italian trademarks and patents, either in absolute terms or as a share of Italian sales. The results for all destination economies in for years 2011, 2012 and 2013 are reported in Table B.4 in Annex B.

In terms of the economies of origin of counterfeit goods that infringe the IP rights of Italian companies, it should be noted that in many sectors the Internet spawns increasingly efficient distribution channels. It is now the main means for matching infringers and consumers. Counterfeiters tend to use both the "big" platforms and marketplaces (eBay, Amazon, etc.), and the smaller fake websites, which can look genuine and advertise digitally on social media.

3.2.2. Which types of Italian products are most susceptible to counterfeiting?

The unified dataset on customs seizures of counterfeit and pirated goods can also be used to discern the product categories in which Italian trademarks and patents are the most vulnerable to global counterfeiting and piracy. Over the period 2011-13, these ranged from basic common goods to luxury or intermediary products (see Figure 3.2).

Figure 3.2. Top categories for fake Italian products, 2011-13

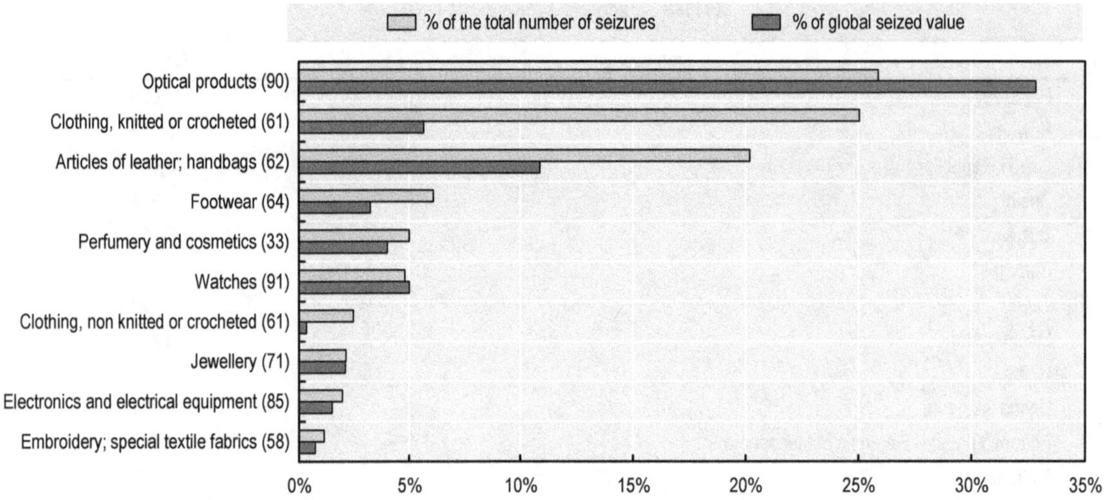

% of the total number of seizures
% of global seized value
Optical products (90)
Clothing, knitted or crocheted (61)
Articles of leather; handbags (62)
Footwear (64)
Perfumery and cosmetics (33)
Watches (91)
Clothing, non knitted or crocheted (61)
Jewellery (71)
Electronics and electrical equipment (85)
Embroidery; special textile fabrics (58)
0% 5% 10% 15% 20% 25% 30% 35%

Note: Figures in parenthesis are Harmonized System (HS) codes as defined by the United Nations Trade Statistics (UN Trade Statistics, 2017).

Importantly, branded products produced by Italian small and medium enterprises are often targeted by counterfeiters. These products can come from various sectors, ranging from agriculture to furniture and luxury apparel products.

Although the scale of production of these firms is limited due do their small size they often offer excellent quality products that are highly reputed. Consequently, they become very profitable targets for counterfeiters, as there are high potential returns from trademark infringements.

In addition, SMEs often do not have sufficient resources and capacities to monitor this threat, and to develop effective countermeasures. The consequences for SMEs can therefore be much more severe than for big companies that have experience and capacities to deal with the risks of counterfeiting (Box 3.1).

Although the scope of goods that are sensitive to IP infringement is broad, the degree to which counterfeiting and piracy target Italian trademarks and patents varies significantly across product categories. Seizures statistics reported in Figure 3.2 below indicate that worldwide Italian-related IPR infringements are especially concentrated in a limited number of industries. Relating to both the number of customs seizures and the seized value, these include sunglasses, clothing, articles of leather and handbags, footwear, perfumery and cosmetics and watches.

The GTRIC-p index is then used to compare which product categories are most likely to be vulnerable to counterfeiting and piracy. For each product category, this index compares global customs seizures intensities of fakes infringing Italy-related IPR with the share of this product category in Italian sales (exports plus domestic sales). The result is a general ranking of industries according to their propensity to contain Italian trademarks or patents that are sensitive to counterfeiting and piracy (Table 3.2; see Table B.5 in Annex B for a complete list).

A high GTRIC-p score implies either that a given product category contains high values of Italian trademarks or patents that are sensitive to global counterfeiting and piracy in absolute terms (e.g. in euros); or, that a large share of the production of goods associated with an Italian trademark or patent registered in this product category is counterfeit or pirated.

Box 3.1. Italian SMEs are at risk!

An example of a small Italian enterprise that suffered from counterfeiting was provided during an interview by an Italian industry association.

Company X was a family business, designing and producing in-house luxury footwear in small quantities in Italy. Given the high quality of products and attractive design, it enjoyed a strong reputation and high demand for their products. Being a very small, family run company, X followed a traditional model of distribution, offering their collections in a selected number of stationary boutiques only.

At one point, company X decided to explore the possibility of opening an in-house, online store. A short analysis revealed the presence of an enormous number of footwear branded X in the on-line e-commerce environment, including the biggest retail platforms. An overwhelming majority of them were counterfeits.

According to the Italian industry association, company X could simply not counter this phenomenon. As the manager of X noted "we are a small, family-run business. We have no means to monitor the Internet. We have no anti-counterfeiting unit, nor even a legal department. Our strength and expertise is in shoemaking. "

Table 3.2. The 15 product categories most sensitive to violation of Italian IPR in global trade

GTRIC-p scores, average 2011-2013

HS category	GTRIC-p
Optical; photographic; medical apparatus (90)	1.000
Watches (91)	1.000
Articles of leather; handbags (42)	1.000
Perfumery and cosmetics (33)	0.995
Clothing and accessories, not knitted or crocheted (62/65)	0.992
Clothing, knitted or crocheted (61)	0.980
Finishing of textiles (58)	0.979
Footwear (64)	0.814
Miscellaneous articles of base metal (83)	0.567
Toys and games (95)	0.438
Jewellery (71)	0.389
Other made-up textile articles (63)	0.337
Knitted or crocheted fabrics (60)	0.280
Electrical machinery and electronics (85)	0.276
Glass and glassware (70)	0.257

Notes: A high GTRIC-p score implies either that a given product category contains high values of Italian trademarks or patents that are sensitive to global counterfeiting and piracy in absolute terms (e.g. in euros); or, that a large share of the production of goods associated with an Italian trademark or patent registered in this product category is counterfeit or pirated. Figures in parenthesis are Harmonized System (HS) codes as defined by the United Nations Trade Statistics (UN Trade Statistics, 2017).

In addition to the types of Italian products targeted for counterfeiting, the number of seizures of fake packaging and logos is growing. This confirms qualitative findings about the domestic assembly of counterfeit and pirated products from imported materials, formulated in structured interviews with Italian enforcement authorities. In terms of overall findings, this calls for conservative interpretation of the final results, as packaging and labels have a significantly lower value than the final products. According to GTRIC methodology, all counterfeit packaging and labels are treated as "packaging", and represent the value of packaging. The fake logos and stickers are then used in the final phase of assembling the fake item, which happens in Italy.

In addition, there are numerous instances of a fake brand name or logo being registered, in China but also within the EU; these are considered to be lookalikes, and are very similar to those of the brands. For example, the term "Raybane" is used to infringe the IP of Ray-Ban.

3.2.3. What is the value of global trade in counterfeit products that infringe Italian IPRs?

As explained in the Step 7 in Annex A.3, applying the GTRIC-e and GTRIC-p indices to data on Italian exports and domestic sales allows the absolute values to be gauged for trade in counterfeit and pirated goods infringing the IPR owned by Italian residents. These absolute values are expressed as upper limits of trade counterfeit and pirated goods, in percentage of exports and sales. To calculate these ceiling values, and to translate the results from relative values to absolute ones (e.g. in monetary terms) it is first necessary to establish a "fixed point". The "fixed point" is the percentage of counterfeit goods in total imports in a selected product category from a given trade partner, for which reliable data are available. The fixed points can be usually established with certain credibility through interviews with enforcement official for the pairs "product category–destination economy" that are the most intense in terms of trade in counterfeit and pirated goods (see OECD/EUIPO (2016) for more discussion).

To verify if values of the "fixed point" determined during the interviews with customs officials and experts result in robust results, some additional checks are carried out. To do so, the empirical application is based on three scenarios, with selected values of 10%, 15% and 20%. Note that all of these scenarios take much more conservative values of fixed points than the actual fixed points applied to imports in OECD/EUIPO (2016).

Table 3.3 below reports the estimated value of global trade in counterfeit products infringing Italian trademarks and patents for years 2011, 2012 and 2013, for these three alternative ceiling values. The best estimates based on the data provided by customs authorities worldwide, and on the GTRIC methodology, indicate that global trade in counterfeit and pirated products infringing Italian trademarks and patents amounted to as much as EUR 35.58 billion in 2013, equivalent to 4.9% of total Italian manufacturing sales (domestic plus exports). This means around 7.7% of global trade in counterfeit and pirated products is related to goods infringing Italian patents or trademarks (EUR 35.6 billion over the EUR 461 billion estimated in the OECD/EUIPO (2016) report).

Table 3.3. Estimated value of global trade in counterfeit products infringing Italian IPR. 2011-13

Year	2011		2012		2013	
Unit	Value in EUR bn	Share of sales	Value in EUR bn	Share of sales	Value in EUR bn	Share of sales
Ceiling value 20%	24.22	3.31%	34.98	4.42%	35.58	4.87%
Ceiling value 15%	18.16	2.49%	26.23	3.32%	26.69	3.37%
Ceiling value 10%	12.44	1.70%	17.49	2.21%	17.79	2.39%

Figure 3.3 breaks down this amount by product category. In absolute terms (i.e. in millions of euros), Italian trademarks and patents related to electronic and electrical equipment, optical products, scientific instruments, machinery and equipment; clothing, footwear and leather, and food products were particularly targeted by counterfeiters and pirates in global trade. In relative terms, articles of leather and handbags, apparel, and perfumery and cosmetics were the most often faked type of products worldwide, with fakes making up more than 11% of all goods within each category.

Figure 3.3. Top product categories subject to infringements of Italian IPR in global trade, 2013

A. In terms of value

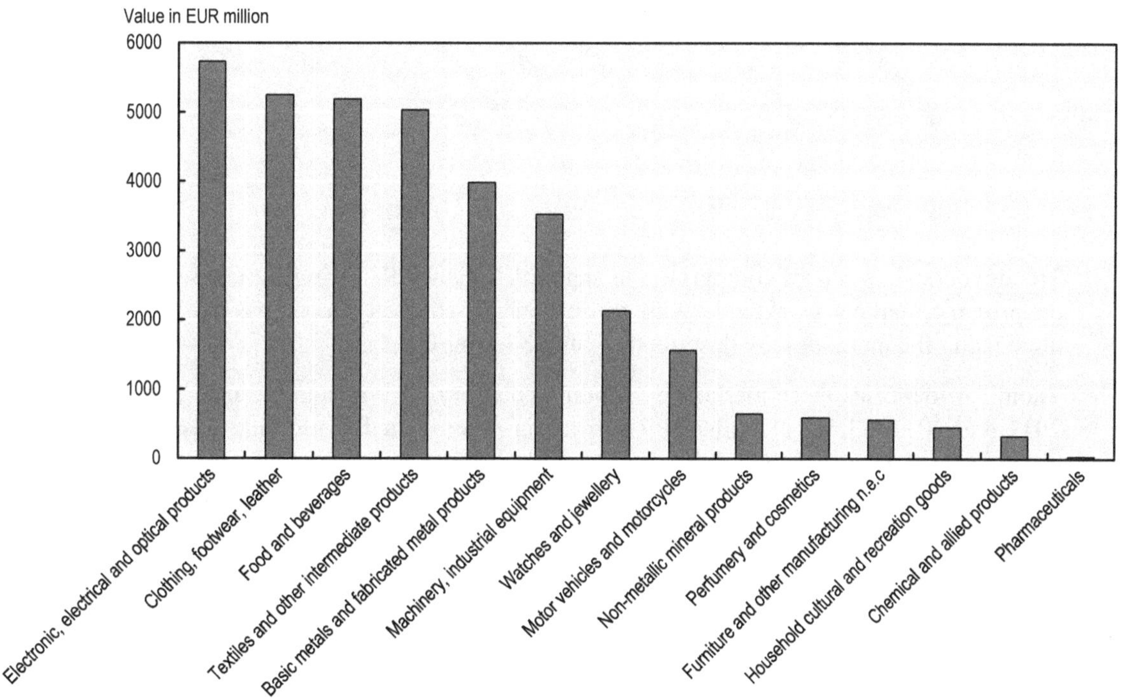

Figure 3.3. Top product categories subject to infringements of Italian IPR in global trade, 2013 (*continued*)

B. In terms of share within the product category

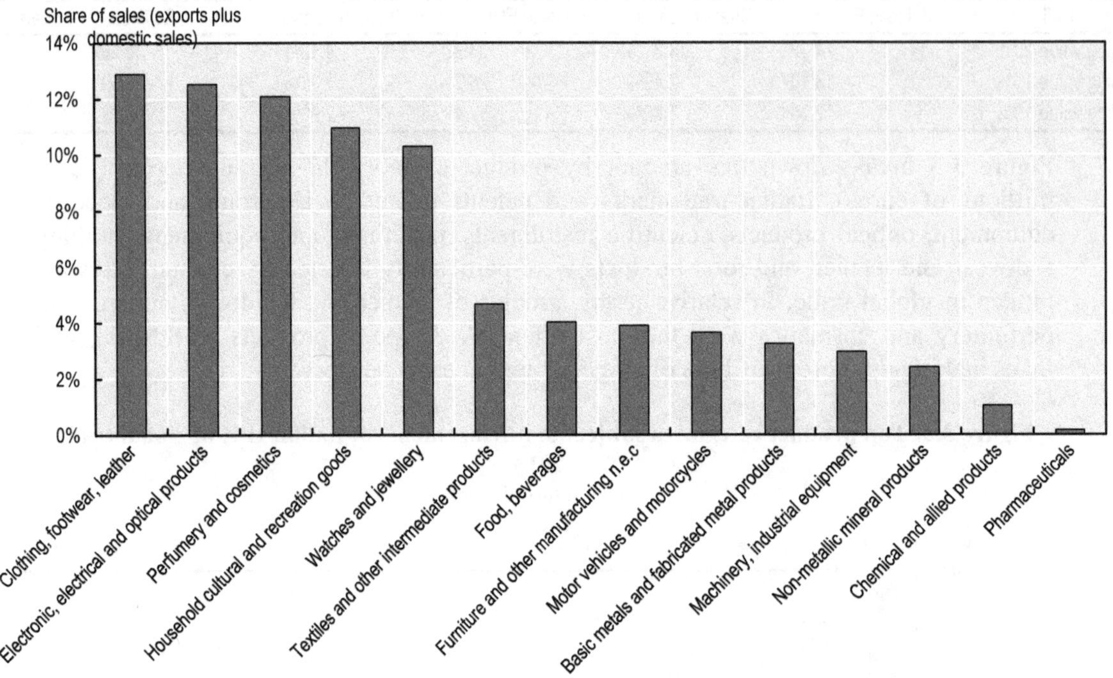

3.3. Primary and secondary markets for counterfeit Italian products

The next step consists of comparing the share of Italian IPR-infringing fakes that are sold on primary markets worldwide with those that are sold on secondary markets. This is done using the methodology described in Step 8 (Annex A.3).

Table 3.4 identifies these markets by product category. The results indicate that between 2011 and 2013, 53.6% of Italian IPR-infringing fakes traded worldwide were offered on secondary markets, i.e. they were openly sold as fakes to consumers. This share varies between product categories, ranging from 14% for foodstuff and beverages and tobacco to 68% for watches and jewellery.

Table 3.4. Share of secondary markets for counterfeit products infringing IPR, 2011-13

Sector	Share of the secondary market
Food, beverages and tobacco	14.35%
Chemical and allied products	15.33%
Pharmaceutical and medicinal chemical products	28.57%
Perfumery and cosmetics	62.61%
Textiles and other intermediate products (e.g. plastics; rubbers; paper; wood)	56.10%
Clothing, footwear, leather and related products	60.02%
Watches and jewellery	68.35%
Non-metallic mineral products (e.g. glass and glass products, ceramic products)	50.00%
Basic metals and fabricated metal products (except machinery and equipment)	27.14%
Electronic and electrical equipment, optical products, scientific instruments	60.03%
Machinery, industrial equipment; computers and peripheral equipment	46.94%
Motor vehicles and motorcycles	65.29%
Household cultural and recreation goods	43.26%
Furniture, lighting equipment, carpets and other manufacturing n.e.c	37.59%
Total	53.62%

It is reported that the Internet has become the main means of matching the infringers and consumers. In this context, some geographical differences merit attention. For example, in some developing countries (e.g. Colombia, Malaysia or Thailand), counterfeit goods that infringed IP of Italian companies tend to be distributed through legitimate channels, and consumers can be deceived by finding them in equally legitimate, "traditional" stores. However, the traditional way of distribution tends to diminish with the increasing availability of counterfeits on the Internet.

In the context of sales of counterfeit goods that infringe Italian IP, it should be stressed that many of these pose very serious health and safety risks for consumers, For example, with respect to counterfeit sunglasses or lenses, some external tests were performed that revealed in particular the three following nonconformities:

- Some fake lenses can affect the ability to recognise colours. This implies that they are not suitable for driving, since the driver will be unable to recognise traffic lights.
- There are also problems with the ability of fake lenses to resist impacts. Fake sunglasses also did not test resistant to impact, and were susceptible to serious corrosion of the frame.
- Fake sunglasses that are not sufficiently resistant can generate allergies for the frame owners and harm the skin.

Counterfeit car components produced originally by Italian manufacturers are another example of fakes that pose serious safety threats to consumers. For example, the high-end car brake producer Brembo reported it had been suffering from counterfeiting, and in many instances fakes could be found on primary markets, appearing the same as the originals Brembo (2015). Most analysed fake brakes were made from poor quality materials that would not pass any quality control, were poorly assembled, and had much lower overall quality levels. Consequently, it is likely that such fake brakes would not function the way original brakes would do, and consequently pose very serious safety risks for users.

It should be highlighted that these health and safety damages cannot be simply quantified, and hence they fall outside the scope of this report.

3.4. The effect of counterfeiting on sales by Italian IPR owners

What value of sales were never realised by Italian right owners due to counterfeiting of their products? This is calculated following the methodology described in Step 9 (Annex A.3).

The total volume of forgone sales by Italian companies due to infringement of their IP rights in 2013 for scenario 1 amounted to EUR 25.1 billion, or 3.1% of their total sales in that year (domestic plus exports). The manufacturing industries for electronics, electrical equipment, and optical and scientific products; and for foodstuff and beverages incurred the highest losses (respectively, EUR 4.6 billion and EUR 4.2 billion of forgone sales in 2013). In terms of shares of sales, the highest losses were recorded by the manufacturing industries for clothing, footwear and leather products; and perfumery and cosmetics, which lost over 8.8% and 8.5% of their sales, respectively

Table 3.5. Estimated lost sales for Italian domestic manufacturing industries, 2013

Sector	Value in EUR mn	Share of sales
Food, beverages and tobacco	4160.97	3.3%
Chemical and allied products	246.82	0.7%
Pharmaceuticals	20.94	0.1%
Perfumery and cosmetics	468.62	8.5%
Textiles and other intermediate products (e.g. plastics; rubbers; paper; wood)	3196.46	2.8%
Clothing, footwear, leather and related products	3534.91	8.8%
Watches and jewellery	1255.37	6.9%
Non-metallic mineral products (e.g. glass and glass products, ceramic products)	400.74	1.4%
Basic metals and fabricated metal products (except machinery and equipment)	2948.71	2.2%
Electronic and electrical equipment, optical products, scientific instruments	4646.64	8.0%
Machinery, industrial equipment; computers and peripheral equipment	2626.64	1.9%
Motor vehicles and motorcycles	920.89	2.0%
Household cultural and recreation goods	318.54	7.6%
Furniture and other manufacturing n.e.c	344.77	1.2%
Total manufacturing sector	25091.02	3.1%

3.5. The effect of counterfeiting on jobs in the Italian manufacturing industry

Lower sales of genuine Italian patented and trademarked products translate into fewer jobs in the Italian manufacturing sectors affected. In order to estimate the amount of jobs lost due to infringement of Italian trademarks and patents in global trade, the basic econometric model presented in Annex A.3 was used. This drew on estimates of the transmission rates (elasticities) between lost sales and lost jobs (Table A.4 in Annex A.3).

Table 3.6 displays the total number of job losses in various branches of the Italian manufacturing industry. Overall, the total number lost due to infringement of Italian trademarks or patents in global trade amounted to more than 64 300, equivalent to 2.4% of the total number of employees in the Italian manufacturing sector.

Table 3.6. Estimated lost jobs in Italian manufacturing industries, 2013

Sector	Number of employees	Share of employees
Food, beverages and tobacco	8510	2.0%
Chemical and allied products	328	0.4%
Pharmaceutical and medicinal chemical products	38	0.1%
Perfumery and cosmetics	673	4.4%
Textiles and other intermediate products	11228	1.8%
Clothing, footwear, leather and related products	17407	5.1%
Watches and jewellery	1091	3.3%
Non-metallic mineral products	1916	0.9%
Basic metals and fabricated metal products	7589	1.1%
Electronic, electrical, and optical products, scientific instruments	7176	4.0%
Machinery, industrial equipment; computers and peripheral equipment	5210	0.8%
Motor vehicles and motorcycles	1516	0.9%
Household cultural and recreation goods	429	4.0%
Furniture and other manufacturing n.e.c	1204	0.5%
Total manufacturing sector	64316	2.4%

Note: Employees are measured in full time equivalent units according to Eurostat (2018)[1] definition.

3.6. The effect of Italian IPR infringement on government revenues

Lower sales and lower profits for Italian rights holders mean they pay lower corporate income tax to the government. In addition, fewer employees mean lower personal income tax revenues and lower social security contributions. Finally, lost sales on the Italian domestic markets mean lower value-added taxes on consumption. In 2013 this forgone tax revenue amounted to EUR 5.9 billion (Table 3.8), equivalent to 1.9% of total Italian public revenues collected on these three taxes.

Table 3.7. Public revenue losses due to Italian IPR infringements in global trade, 2013

Tax type	Value in EUR mn	Share
PIT and SSC	2616.9	1.5%
Corporate taxes	1730.9	4.2%
Value added taxes	1508.6	1.6%
Total	5856.4	1.9%

References

Brembo (2015), New Anti-Counterfeiting Car Will Protect Buyers of Brembo High Perforance and Racing Products, Brembo S.p.A, Curno (Bergamo), http://www.brembo.com/en/company/news/brembo-puts-the-brakes-on-counterfeit-products (accessed on 26 February 2018).

Eurostat (2018), Structural Business Statistics, Statistical office of the European Union, Luxembourg, http://ec.europa.eu/eurostat/cache/metadata/fr/sbs_esms.htm (last accessed on May 2018)

OECD/EUIPO (2016), *Trade in Counterfeit and Pirated Goods: Mapping the Economic Impact*, OECD Publishing, Paris, http://dx.doi.org/10.1787/9789264252653-en.

UN Trade Statistics (2017), Harmonized commodity description and coding systems (HS), United Nations, Geneva, https://unstats.un.org/unsd/tradekb/Knowledgebase/50018/Harmonized-Commodity-Description-and-Coding-Systems-HS

Notes

[1] Eurostat (2018) defines employees as those persons who work for an employer and who have a contract of employment and receive compensation in the form of wages, salaries, fees, gratuities, piecework pay or remuneration in kind. A worker from an employment agency is considered to be an employee of that temporary employment agency and not of the unit (customer) in which they work.

4. What is the impact on Italy overall?

This study presents the direct, economic effects of counterfeiting on Italian consumers, the Italian retail and manufacturing industry, and the Italian government. The findings of this study should assist public and private decision-makers in formulating effective, cohesive, and evidence-based responses to this risk. In addition, the methodology developed for this report could be re-used to determine the scale of harm caused by counterfeiting on the Italian economy on a regular basis.

4.1. Trade in fake goods: The overall impact on Italy

This report has assessed quantitatively the value and scope of trade in counterfeit and pirated products in Italy, and gauged some of its effect on consumers, jobs, sales and tax revenue in that country.

It looked at two particular categories of effects: those of imports of counterfeit and pirated products in Italy; and those of global trade in Italian IPR-infringing products. Adding together the results gives a good idea of the overall impact of counterfeit trade on Italian consumers, right holders and government.[1]

Concerning the total impact of counterfeit trade in Italy, the best available statistics show that the total consumer detriment due to consumer deception by counterfeiters in 2013 amounted to almost EUR 2 billion. The sales losses to Italian wholesale and retail industries in 2013 amounted to EUR 23.6 billion, or 4.1% of total sales in that year. The total volume of forgone sales by Italian rights owners due to infringement of their IP in 2013 amounted to EUR 55.5 billion, or 4.4% of their total sales in that year. These sale losses subsequently translate into lost jobs and lower tax returns (Table 4.1).

Table 4.1. Total direct impact of counterfeit and pirated trade in the Italian context, 2013

Total lost sales (wholesale and retail)		Total lost sales (Italian IP right owners)		Total lost jobs		Total lost taxes	
EUR 6.9 billion	2.7% of sales	EUR 25.1 billion	3.1% of sales	87800 lost jobs	1.97% of full time equivalent employees	EUR 9.6 billion	0.9% of Italian GDP

An assessment of the global damage due to counterfeiting and piracy on the Italian economy can be made by comparing the scale of losses due to counterfeiting in Italy on the one hand, and due to infringement of IP rights of Italian firms on the other hand.

It absolute terms, losses experienced due to infringement of Italian IP abroad are much greater than those due to imports of fakes to Italy. In terms of damage to Italian revenue they amounted to EUR 5.9 billion of foregone taxes vs EUR 3.7 billion caused by imports of fakes to Italy. This calls for continued strong involvement of Italy in international, plurilateral and multilateral initiatives to counter the risk of trade in counterfeit and pirated goods.

It seems that there are two main reasons, why the impact of infringement of Italian IP abroad is much more devastating than the imports of fakes to Italy:

- Firstly, products offered by Italian companies are particularly attractive for counterfeiters due to their innovativeness, high quality and the great reputation they enjoy. It means that globally, trade in counterfeit and pirated goods poses a vital threat to Italian companies that can undermine their innovative efforts and investment.
- Secondly, Italy has a strong governance response system that seems to be effective in reducing the overall damage of counterfeit imports to Italy, and temper the demand for fakes in Italy. This is confirmed by several studies that report very low tolerance for fakes among Italian consumers (EUIPO, 2017).

In addition, many fake products sold in Italy are electrical and electronic components that are often sold on primary markets to unaware consumers. These products that are offered by parties that do not respect warranties; the products themselves often pose significant health and safety risks to unaware consumers, as documented by several studies (UL, 2016). It also means that the intergovernmental co-ordination of anti-counterfeiting efforts is essential to take into account those impacts that might be within the scope of all relevant agencies (e.g. those in charge of health and safety or environmental impacts).

Regarding IP infringement of Italian products worldwide, it should be also noted that many infringed products are produced by Italian small and medium enterprises. These products in most cases enjoy great reputation, and consequently become very profitable targets for counterfeiters. At the same time SMEs often do not have sufficient resources and capacities to monitor this threat, and to develop effective countermeasures. It means that the negative impacts for SMEs can be much more severe than for big companies that have experience and capacities to deal with the risks of counterfeiting. This reinforces the call for stronger co-operation in international actions against the trade in fakes.

Overall, this report has presented a state-of-the-art quantitative analysis of the scale of counterfeiting in the Italian context, and of its negative impacts in areas such as jobs, consumer detriment and public revenue. The study developed a methodology to gauge the magnitude and scale of counterfeit trade in Italy and to quantify its direct economic impact. It relied primarily on a unique international set of customs seizure data, as well as structured interviews with trade and customs experts.

In particular, the best available estimates based on the customs data indicate that global counterfeiting and piracy in 2013 resulted in almost 87 800 lost jobs in Italy. That same year, counterfeit trade resulted in almost EUR 26 billion of forgone tax revenue for the Italian Government.

The magnitude of the issue, and the scale of its impact, should remain of high priority to both Italian policy makers and the country's private sector. There are significant implications for the future, including those for activities that generate high value-added, and those for innovation potential, both of which are sources of long-term economic growth.

4.2. Improving the evidence

Even though information on counterfeit and pirated trade has significantly improved in recent years, it still falls far short of what is needed for robust analysis that can serve as the basis for more granular conclusions. Further research on measurement techniques and data collection methods could help refine the analysis and close data gaps. The key data-related issues identified in this study refer to:

- lack of compatibility and completeness of existing datasets, which calls for greater harmonisation of data collection
- information gaps on consumer behaviour, especially on substitution rates, which calls for more surveys and experiments
- difficulties in quantifying certain impacts of counterfeiting, e.g. the effects on consumers' health and safety, which calls for more co-ordinated efforts.

Regarding the lack of compatibility and completeness of existing datasets, existing datasets and frameworks for data collection could be used more fully for improving our understanding of the many aspects of counterfeiting and piracy. Unfortunately, as the analysis revealed, these datasets and the frameworks for data collection are often inconsistent or incomplete.

As different taxonomies have been used to create individual datasets, they are often incompatible. Trying to match them can be very laborious or even impossible. For example, on the one hand datasets on counterfeit seizures were created from the trade-related taxonomies (such as the World Customs Organization [WCO]'s Harmonized System), while data on industrial activity rely on the *International Standard Industrial Classification* of All Economic Activities (ISIC) categorisation. Matching these essentially incompatible datasets could provide a wealth of additional information, for example about the production points of counterfeit products.

To address this issue, more consistency is needed in data collection and harmonisation processes. For example the Customs Enforcement Network (CEN), a reporting framework developed by customs agencies through the World Customs Organization (WCO), offers one of the most promising ways forward for improving information on infringement of counterfeit and pirated products. The framework establishes the parameters for reporting on seized/intercepted products. The Harmonized System of the WCO, for example, provides a coded nomenclature for over 5 200 items; using this at the detailed six-digit level would provide much-needed specificity about the products being intercepted/seized.

In addition to the further development and harmonisation of existing datasets, far more can and should be done to address the information gaps concerning consumer behaviour and to improve understanding of that behaviour as it relates to the purchase of counterfeit goods. This in particular refers to the estimation of substitution rates, which are critical when analysing the effects of counterfeiting and piracy on rights holders, but difficult to develop using traditional economic and econometric tools.

There are two basic ways to assess the substitution rate: surveys and economic experiments. Irrespective of the method chosen, the assumptions underlying approaches should be clear, as should the economic arguments; transparency is key. Outcomes should be evaluated in terms of reasonableness and, wherever possible, be subject to sensitivity analysis to determine how variations in key assumptions affect outcomes.

There are several areas of counterfeiting and counterfeit trade for which no clear or commonly agreed methodology exists to gauge impacts, and so quantifying certain impacts becomes difficult. These include environmental harm due to the use of poor-quality counterfeit chemicals, and adverse effects of counterfeits on consumers' health and safety.

On that last point, there are numerous anecdotal reports on the adverse effects counterfeit products can have on public health and safety or on the environment. Those reports, however, are limited in scope. A more systematic and extensive approach for developing data in this area is therefore needed – a suggestion already made by an OECD report on the economic impact of counterfeiting and piracy OECD (2008). The report presented a potential way of developing information on counterfeit medicine following (Liang et al., 2007). Under a "Patient Safety Reporting System", patients, medical practitioners and suppliers would provide input. Reporting would thereby not be restricted to professionals and rights holders, but would include consumers. To facilitate reporting, it was recommended that provisions be available for supplying input by email, the Internet (via web-based forms), mail or fax. While the focus of the system was directed exclusively towards pharmaceuticals, it could be adapted for use more widely.

Some progress is being made on collecting data on effects in a more systematic fashion, particularly in the pharmaceuticals sector. An International Medical Products Anti-

Counterfeiting Taskforce (IMPACT) was recently created by the World Health Organization (WHO, 2011). Among other goals, the task force aims to develop accessible and reliable information on the nature and extent of the problem. IMPACT has simplified the process and tools for reporting counterfeit medicine, and data collection is now facilitated by the Rapid Alert System (RAS) (WHO, 2013), a web-based reporting platform accessible to any interested party.

4.3. Next steps

The unique methodology developed for this report can lend itself to a number of additional exercises. These could include other country studies, which could eventually lead to a benchmarking exercise. The potential for additional case studies is particularly fruitful where the data are abundant and where there is evidence of significant impact by infringements.

The methodology could also be successfully and repetitively re-applied to determine the relative changes in the scale and effects of counterfeiting and piracy in Italy. In addition, the methodology offers some flexibility in accommodate improvements in research, for example on substitution rates. This could lead to a more detailed analysis that would produce a more complete picture of trade in counterfeit and pirated goods, and its negative impact on rights holders, governments and consumers in Italy.

References

Liang, B. et al. (2007), "The Patient Safety and Quality Improvement Act of 2005: Provisions and Potential Opportunities", *American Journal of Medical Quality*, Vol. 22/1, pp. 8-12.

OECD (2008), *The Economic Impact of Counterfeiting and Piracy*, OECD Publishing, Paris, http:// http://www.oecd.org/sti/ind/theeconomicimpactofcounterfeitingandpiracy.htm.

UL (2016), "Counterfeit iPhone adapters", UL, Montreal,
http://library.ul.com/wp-content/uploads/sites/40/2016/09/10314-CounterfeitiPhone-WP-HighRes_FINAL.pdf.

WHO (2011), *International Medical Products Anti-Counterfeiting Taskforce (IMPACT): The Handbook. Facts, Activities, Documents Developed by the Assembly and the Working Groups, 2006-2010*, World Health Organization, Geneva, http://apps.who.int/medicinedocs/en/d/Js20967en/.

WHO (2013), *WHO Global Surveillance and Monitoring System*, World Trade Organization, Geneva, http://www.who.int/medicines/regulation/ssffc/surveillance/en/.

Notes

[1] Note that the methodology takes into account the "double-counting" issue, which arises from importing fake products into Italy that infringe the IPR of Italian firms. This is done by breaking down the seizure dataset and identifying Italy as the economy of residence of rights holders whose IP rights were infringed. In addition, the framework looks only at areas where quantification was possible; the impact should definitely not be interpreted as the total impact of counterfeit trade in Italy.

Annex A. Methodological notes

A.1. The data

Precise quantification and measurement of the losses to Italian consumers, retail and wholesale industry and government attributable to counterfeit products smuggled into Italy and to infringements of Italian residents' IPR in global trade can prove elusive. This is because the clandestine and illicit nature of counterfeiting means the available data is likely to fall far short of what is needed for robust analysis and policy making (Box A.1). Put differently, the point of departure for any quantitative analysis in the area of counterfeit trade is to establish the sort of statistical data available for analysing the issue.

Box A.1. Data limitations

It is important to highlight that the data on counterfeiting and piracy are scarce and incomplete. Even though some progress in data collection has been observed over recent years, the quality of available statistics on counterfeiting and piracy still needs significant improvement. Consequently, there are three things that should be kept in mind when developing and applying a methodological framework to quantify the effects of counterfeit trade.

1. The framework developed here does not claim to quantify all the impacts of counterfeit and pirated trade on the Italian economy. It looks at areas where quantification was possible, while identifying areas of work needed to better understand how counterfeit and pirated trade affects economies and societies overall.
2. In areas where quantification was possible, the framework relies on a set of methodological assumptions. For transparency purposes, all are clearly spelt out in the text.
3. The framework leaves scope for further methodological amendments subject to future data improvements, for example more precise gauging of consumers' substitution rates between fake and genuine goods.

This report required three types of data, each discussed in the sections that follow:

- seizures data of IP-infringing products from customs and police forces (IPERICO and OECD/EUIPO (2016) on global customs seizures)
- import statistics
- other data – including on consumer behaviour regarding counterfeit products – and other background micro- and macroeconomic data.

Data on seizures of counterfeit products smuggled in Italy

The best information available on counterfeit product smuggling in Italy comes from the IPERICO database (see Box A.2). Information regarding infringements of Italian residents' IPR in global trade are extracted from the database on customs seizures of IP infringing products worldwide presented in the OECD/EUIPO (2016) report.

Box A.2. The IPERICO database

The IPERICO (Intellectual Property – Elaborated Report of the Investigation on Counterfeiting) database gathers information on seizures made by the Italian police forces that work to combat counterfeiting under the guidance of the Ministry of Economic Development, Directorate-General for the Fight against Counterfeiting – Italian Patent and Trademark Office (DGLC-UIBM), with the support of a pool of experts of the Guardia di Finanza, the Agenzia delle Dogane (Customs), and the Criminal Analysis Service of the Home Office.

The original dataset relies on data entries collected and processed by customs and police officers, and as with any other administrative data, they needed careful consideration before use in this quantitative analysis. In particular, harmonisation of the customs agency and tax police databases has led to the creation of a unique database, which merges data produced by both organisations. A set of limitations related to the creation of this unique dataset, including product classification levels and valuations, were carefully addressed by the DGLC-UIBM; these are summarised in their latest reports.

As a result, the database contains a wealth of information about IPR-infringing goods smuggled into Italy and can be used for detailed quantitative and qualitative analysis. In most cases it reports general information, such as the date of seizure, the region where the goods were seized, the provenance economy in the case of customs seizures and the product category, as well as more detailed descriptions, such as the name of the legitimate brand owner, the number of seized products and their estimated value.

Source: http://www.uibm.gov.it/iperico

It should be highlighted that the information contained in the IPERICO and the OECD/EUIPO (2016) databases refers to anti-counterfeiting activities and not to the phenomenon of counterfeiting itself. They may not therefore be considered a direct measurement of the phenomenon with a certifiable statistical value.

It follows that the first step in both analysis developed below consists in gauging the actual value of counterfeit products smuggled into Italy (Step 1) and the actual value of infringements of Italian brands and patents in global trade (Step 7) as carefully as possible. This is done on the basis of the strength and limitations of the IPERICO and the OECD/EUIPO (2016) databases, and the GTRIC methodology developed in OECD/EUIPO (2016).

Import statistics

Italian import statistics used in this report are based on the United Nations (UN) Comtrade database UN Trade Statistics (2018). With 171 reporting economies and 247 partner economies, the database is considered the most comprehensive trade database available. Import statistics are compiled from the records filed with Italian customs authorities. This is particularly important for this report, as all data related to trade and used in the statistical exercise (imports and data on customs seizures of infringing products) originate from the same source: customs offices at the destination.

Within the UN Comtrade database, products are registered on a six-digit Harmonized System (HS) basis UN Trade Statistics (2017), meaning that the level of detail is high.

However, this also signals the creation of a unique taxonomy that allows merging those data on imports of genuine goods with data on seizures of counterfeit goods included in the IPERICO database. It follows that the impact analysis conducted in this report will be performed for the following product categories: clothing, footwear, leather and related products; perfumes, cosmetics and other body care items; computers and computer equipment; electrical and electronic equipment; toys, games and sporting articles; watches and jewellery; other goods.

All correspondence tables between this unique taxonomy, the HS classification system, and the product categories defined in the context of the IPERICO database are presented in the Annex B.

Additional data

Other statistical information was used to develop a methodology to gauge the economic impact of trade in fake goods. This includes:

- statistical information on Italian sectorial production, sales, jobs, and wages, extracted from the Eurostat database Eurostat (2018). Correspondence tables between the classification of economic activities for manufacturing and wholesale and retail industries used by Eurostat (NACE) and the Harmonized System (HS) classification, which is used to calculate both infringements of Italian IPR in global trade and fake imports in Italy, are provided in Annex B.
- statistical information on Italian taxes extracted from the OECD TAX database OECD (2018).
- information on consumers' substitution rates (see below) between genuine goods and fake goods contained in various academic studies and consumer surveys.

A more detailed discussion of these datasets is presented later in this annex.

A.2. Gauging the direct effects of fake goods smuggled into Italy

The impact areas of fake goods smuggled into Italy, as described in chapter 2, can be calculated following a number of steps (Figure A.1):

1. estimating the value of counterfeit products smuggled into Italy
2. estimating the value of those products sold in the primary and secondary markets
3. estimating consumer detriment
4. estimating lost sales for retailers and wholesalers
5. estimating job losses in the retail and wholesale sector
6. estimating taxes forgone

Figure A.1. Steps involved in analysing the economic effects of counterfeit imports in Italy

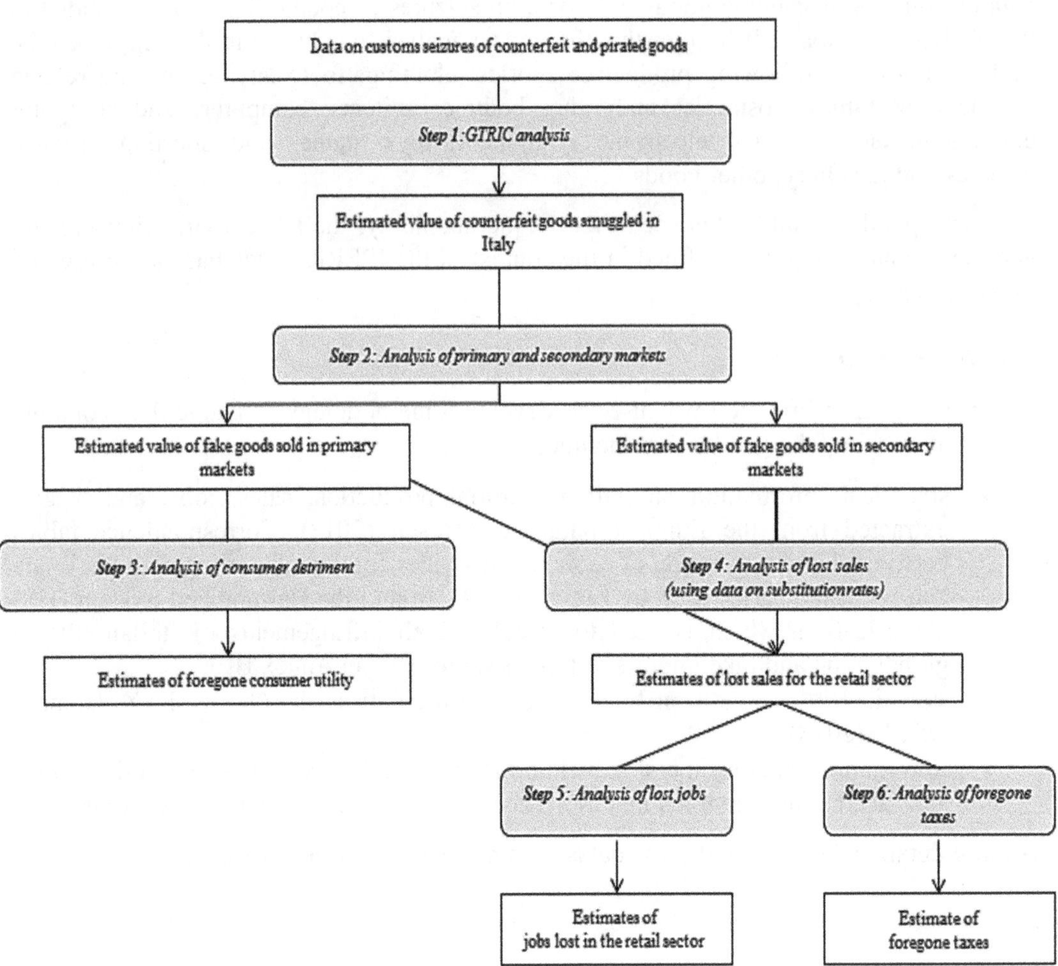

Step 1: Estimating the value of imports of counterfeit and pirated products

This first step involves tailoring the databases on customs seizures of IP-infringing products and on imports of genuine goods, to estimate the value of counterfeit imports in Italy by product category and provenance economy. This partial dataset will then form the basis for the following impact analysis.

The main task of this step is to apply the General Trade-Related Index of Counterfeiting (GTRIC) methodology developed in OECD/EUIPO (2016) to the database of customs seizures in order to gauge the value of fake goods smuggled in Italy, for each product category and provenance economy identified. The GTRIC methodology allows the Italian trade-specific context to be taken into account, and relies on two key econometric components (see Annex A.4 and OECD/EUIPO, 2016 for more detail):

- The GTRIC indices for economies (GTRIC-e) and for products (GTRIC-p). GTRIC-e is an index that ranks economies according to their relative likelihood to being an economy of provenance for counterfeit products smuggled into Italy. GTRIC-p is an index of industries according to their relative proneness to being targeted by counterfeiting.

- The GTRIC matrix, obtained by combining GTRIC-e and GTRIC-p. This matrix assigns a relative probability for each given type of product imported from a given provenance economy to be subject of counterfeiting as compared to the most vulnerable "product category-economy" pair.

Importantly, two assumptions are made to calculate the GTRIC vectors. The first is that the volume of seizures of a given product or from a given source economy is positively correlated with the actual frequency of imports of counterfeit goods in this product category or from that economy. The second assumption acknowledges that this relationship is not linear, as there may be biases in the detection and seizure procedures. For instance, the fact that infringing goods are detected more frequently in certain categories by customs or police forces could imply that differences in counterfeiting factors across products merely reflect that some goods are easier to detect than others – or that some goods, for one reason or another, have been specially targeted for inspection.

While the GTRIC matrix does not provide a direct measure of the overall magnitude of counterfeit imports, it establishes statistical relationships that are useful for this purpose. More specifically, applying the GTRIC matrix to statistics on imports of genuine products allows the upper limit value of counterfeit goods smuggled into Italy to be gauged.

Similar to the approach used in OECD/EUIPO (2016), the approach here establishes an upper limit of counterfeiting (in percentages of imports) for the key "provenance economy-product category" pairs that are the most vulnerable to counterfeiting, i.e. with the highest relative likelihood of being counterfeit (highest GTRIC score). Following OECD/EUIPO (2016), these values are called "fixed points".

In their main report on counterfeit trade, the OECD and EUIPO (2016) gauged six points for a range of six "product category-provenance" pairs where shares of counterfeit products are highest, based on a focus group meeting and on interviews with customs officials. The results were refined using a set of supplementary data on seizures in dedicated actions provided by the European Anti-Fraud Office (OLAF).

Once established, the fixed points combined with the relative probabilities included in the GTRIC matrix allow the share of fake products contained in every "product category-provenance economy" pair to be determined. These shares are then applied to existing statistics on imports of genuine products to estimate the total value of counterfeit imports in Italy.

Step 2: Estimating the value of fake goods sold in the primary and secondary markets

Two questions are crucial in assessing the economic impact of imports of counterfeit and pirated products in Italy for domestic retail and wholesale industry, consumers, and the government. First, what is the proportion of these counterfeit products that are sold on primary versus secondary markets in Italy? Second, within secondary markets, what is the rate at which Italian consumers are substituting counterfeit goods for legitimate products?

Regarding the first question, every sale of a fake item on a primary market clearly represents a direct loss for the retail and wholesale industry. In secondary markets, however, only a share of consumers would have deliberately substituted their purchases of counterfeit products for legitimate ones, because they know that what they are buying is fake. The key issue then is how to calculate the consumers' substitution rate, i.e. the extent to which every knowing illegal purchase displaces a legal sale.

Estimating the share of fakes sold on primary and secondary markets

In order to distinguish fake products counterfeiters intended to sell on the primary market from those intended for sale on the secondary market, the price gap between both types of fakes is calculated. For each seizure specified in the database, Italian customs authorities report the declared value of goods, the quantity seized, the product's HS code, and the infringed trademark. This allows the unit value of each seized "product type-brand" pair (*brand* would include the associated trademark or patent) to be determined. These unit values can then serve as a proxy for the retail prices of the fake goods.

For each type of product associated with a given trademark or patent, the prices of seized goods are used to estimate a confidence interval that contains the actual retail price of the corresponding genuine item. Counterfeit items whose unit price, calculated as described above, are higher than or included in this interval are then classified as intended for sale on the primary market. Those whose price is below this interval are classified as targeting the secondary market.

Formally, let $\mathrm{s_c}$ and $\bar{\mathrm{s}}_\mathrm{c}$ denote, respectively, the import value and quantity of any custom seizure of counterfeit products, with $c \in \{1, \dots, N\}$ the range of customs seizures, and N their total number. $p_c = s_c/\bar{s}_c$ then refers to the unit value of each custom seizure, and can serve as a proxy for their unit price. Let $p_{bp} = \left(\sum_{c\in\{bp\}} p_c\right)/N_{bp}$ defines the (unweighted) price average of any type of product p associated with the brand or patent b, with N_{bp} the total number of custom seizures reported for this "product category - brand" combination. The standard deviation of this price is denoted σ_{bp} .

X_c is defined as a dichotomous (binary) variable that takes the value of 0 if the fake goods included in the seized shipment were intended to be sold on the primary market, or 1 if they were intended to be sold on the secondary market. In accordance with the arguments mentioned in the main text, X_c is assumed to be defined as follows:

$$X_c = \begin{cases} = 0 \text{ if } p_c \in \left[p_{bp} - \dfrac{1.96 \times \sigma_{bp}}{\sqrt{N_{bp}}};\ \max\limits_{c\epsilon\{bp\}} p_c \right] \\ = 1 \text{ if } p_c \in \left[\min\limits_{c\epsilon\{bp\}} p_c;\ p_{bp} - \dfrac{1.96 \times \sigma_{bp}}{\sqrt{N_{bp}}} \right[\end{cases}; \qquad \forall c\{bp\}$$

It follows that the share of products sold on the primary market can be calculated by product category, τ_p^1, and/or for the entire mass of fake imports, and is given by:

$$\tau_p^1 = \left(\sum_b \sum_c x_c s_c\right) / \left(\sum_b \sum_c s_c\right), \quad \forall c\epsilon\{bp\}$$

For example, Figure A.2 shows the price distribution of fake Rolex watches produced that were seized by Italian customs between 2011 and 2013. Using the methodology outlined indicates that most fake Rolex watches with prices lower than EUR 250 were destined for the secondary market, while those with values higher than EUR 250 (observations in the middle and on the right hand side of the distribution) were targeted at the primary market.

Figure A.2. Price distribution of fake Rolex watches seized by Italian customs, 2011-2013

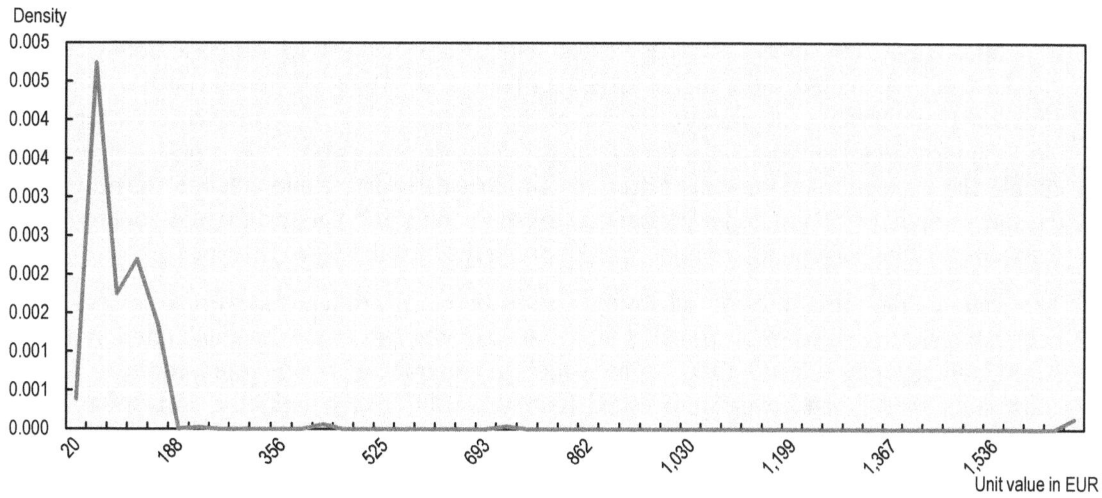

Substitution rates on secondary markets

In primary markets, consumers pay the full retail price for a fake product thinking it is the genuine article. The assumption can be made that a legitimate item would have been bought in the absence of the fake product. This represents a one-to-one substitution rate (a 100% displacement rate), and therefore a one-to-one direct loss for the industry. Note that this one-to-one substitution rate requires three important conditions: 1) the consumer is paying full retail price (or near enough) for the fake product; 2) the consumer is not aware they are purchasing a counterfeit product; and 3) the fake good is almost identical in appearance to the genuine one.

In secondary markets, consumers knowingly purchase IP-infringing products. The issue then is to estimate the likelihood that consumers would have purchased the genuine product at its full price. Clearly, these substitution rates vary by industry and economy, since factors such as product quality, distribution channels, and information available about the product can differ significantly. They also depend on the consumer's motives for purchasing counterfeit and pirated goods. For example, some consumers buy counterfeits for fun, which may not provide any guidance on specific values to use.

As mentioned previously, the substitution rate is the assumed rate at which a consumer is willing to switch from purchasing a fake good to the genuine product. In other words, this displacement analysis seeks to identify the extent to which consumers substitute purchases of counterfeit and pirated products for legitimate ones. The main goal is to identify sales that were never realised by industries due to counterfeiting and piracy. Formally, a displacement rate of $x\%$ means that every $100/x$ illegal purchases of a given counterfeit product displace a legal sale.

Information on substitution rates can be obtained from two different sources: academic research on consumers' socio-economic behaviour, and consumer surveys. The majority of academic research, however, has focused on intangible pirated products, such as digital piracy.

Findings are rarer for tangible products, with the exception of luxury items. For example, Yoo and Lee (2009) studied the behaviour of Korean female college students and found a substitution rate of 21% for luxury fashion clothing and accessories.

In another study, consumers were presented with an opportunity to purchase counterfeit products in a simulated shopping experience (Tom et al., 1998). When given the choice between a counterfeit or legitimate version of the product, 32% of the consumers selected the counterfeit version and 68% opted for the legitimate version.[1,2] The preference for counterfeit or legitimate versions differs by product category. Counterfeit T-shirts were the most popular (42% stated a preference for the counterfeit version), while counterfeit software was the least popular (17% stated a preference for the fake software).

The issue of the variability of substitution rates between product categories has barely been addressed in consumer surveys. One of the exceptions is a survey conducted by the Anti-Counterfeiting Group (2007), in which a sample of 1 003 representative UK consumers aged 16 and over were asked if they would have bought the corresponding legitimate item had the fake item not been available Anti-Counterfeiting Group (2007). Among this sample, 39% responded that they would have bought a genuine alternative (either made by the brand or another brand) in the case of clothing or footwear products, 49% in the case of fragrance, and 27% in the case of watches.[3]

Given the scarcity of data, the empirical exercise performed in Chapter 2 relies on three different scenarios. The first scenario assumes substitution rates that follow the results of the Anti-Counterfeiting Group (2007)'s consumer survey. In this scenario, a substitution rate of 39% has been chosen for the product category relating to clothing and footwear – meaning that every EUR 2.5 spent on fake clothes, accessories or footwear in secondary markets translates into EUR 1 in lost sales for the retail and wholesale industry. Also in accordance with this consumer survey, the selected rates in scenario 1 are 49% for products relating to the perfumery and cosmetics sector, and 27% for products belonging to the watch and jewellery industries. Finally, according to the study carried out by Tom et al. (1998), the selected substitution rate is 32% for all other fake products sold on secondary markets. The second scenario is more conservative, and assumes substitution rates 10 percentage points lower. The third scenario is the most conservative; it assumes the substitution rates to be 20 percentage points lower than in the first scenario.

In order to test the robustness of the results, the estimates of lost sales, lost jobs and lost taxes thus rely on three alternative scenarios, based on lower assumed consumers' substitution rates. These are presented in Section A.6 of this Annex A.

Step 3: Estimating consumer detriment

Individual consumer detriment is the price premium unjustly paid by the consumer in the belief they are buying a genuine product. As consumers who choose to purchase counterfeit products on secondary markets deliberately accept a cost-quality trade-off, consumer detriment only occurs in primary markets. For each product category the individual consumer detriment is estimated by calculating the difference between the average price paid in the primary market (by deceived consumers) and that paid in the secondary market (by consumers who knowingly buy fake goods). This individual consumer detriment is then multiplied by the total volume of transactions in the primary market in a given product category. Finally, for all product categories the detriments are added together to give a general estimate of overall consumer detriment.

More formally, the principle behind the measure of consumer detriment is as follows. First, for any type of product p related to the brand b, the average price paid on primary market, p_{bp}^{1}, and the average price paid on secondary market, p_{bp}^{2}, are calculated. Since the gap between these prices represents the "value of consumers' deception", it can be used as a proxy for consumer detriment of purchasing a given branded product bp on the primary market: $d_{bp} = p_{bp}^{1} - p_{bp}^{2}$. Finally, these detriments can be aggregated by product category, or at the national level, multiplying them by the estimated volume of sales on primary markets, Q_{bp}^{1}, as follows: $D = \sum_b \sum_p \left(d_{bp} Q_{bp}^{1}\right)$.

Step 4: Estimating lost sales for retailers and wholesalers

In order to measure lost sales for retailers and wholesalers due to counterfeit products, three sets of information are used:

1. The estimated value of counterfeit products smuggled into Italy by product category, as obtained in Step 1.
2. The shares of primary and secondary markets, which are estimated at the most detailed level (ideally by brand and product type) using the methodology described in the first part of Step 2.
3. Information on consumers' substitution rates, which are extracted from consumer surveys, as explained in the second part of Step 2.

The estimated value of counterfeit products smuggled into Italy combined with the share of the primary market gives the total volume of lost sales for Italian retailers and wholesalers due to the unsuspecting purchase of counterfeit products. The estimated value of counterfeit goods smuggled into Italy, combined with the shares of the secondary market and consumers' substitution rates, equals the total volume of lost sales for Italian retailers and wholesalers due to the knowing purchase of counterfeit products. This takes into account the fact that those consumers would not necessarily have bought the genuine alternatives if the fakes had not been available. Finally, the sum of both estimates reveals the total value of lost sales for wholesalers and retailers due to counterfeit imports.

Formally, for each product type p, the loss of sales incurred by domestic wholesalers and retailers due to counterfeit and pirated imports, S_p, is given by adding the estimated value of counterfeit and pirated imports sold on the primary market – i.e. the total value of counterfeit and pirated imports, C_p (estimated in Step 1), times the share of the primary market, τ_p^1 (estimated in Step 2) – to the estimated value of fakes sold on the secondary market times the consumers' substitution rates, ρ_p:

$$S_p = \left[\tau_p^1 \times C_p\right] + \left[(1 - \tau_p^1) \times C_p \times \rho_p\right]$$

Step 5: Estimating job losses in the retail and wholesale sector

Estimates of lost jobs for each Italian retail and wholesale industries are based on two key factors: (i) the share of lost sales as calculated in Step 4; and (ii) the transmission rates between lost sales and lost jobs for each industry, which are calculated as presented below.

Transmission rates between lost sales and jobs in Italian wholesale and retail industries

The economic literature does not make clear links between the values of lost sales and lost jobs for each industry. This study therefore developed a simple econometric model to address that issue. The aim is to explain the extent to which the retail and wholesale industry adjusts employment when sales vary.

The idea behind the model is to invert a basic production function in a partial equilibrium model in order to estimate the response of employment to a sales shock. $\hat{p}_p$ and $\hat{Q}_P$ can denote, respectively, the average unit price and the total production in volume of (genuine) goods in industry p, so that the total sales of (genuine) goods in an industry is defined by

$$\hat{S}_p = \hat{p}_p \times \hat{Q}_P$$

The goods in the industry are produced using labour, $\hat{L}_p$, capital $\hat{K}_p$, and intermediate inputs $\hat{I}_p$, following a Cobb-Douglas production:

$$\hat{Q}_P = A_p \, \hat{L}_p^{\alpha} \, \hat{K}_p^{\beta} \, \hat{I}_p^{\gamma}$$

with A_p the total factor productivity (TFP). In accordance with traditional economic literature, the firms' profit maximisation problem within an industry yield an optimal price which equalises a markup φ_p, over a marginal cost, here the productivity-adjusted wage w_p :

$$\hat{p}_p = \varphi_p \, w_p$$

Combining the three equations above and taking the log yields:

$$\ln(\hat{S}_p) = \ln(\varphi_p) + \ln(w_p) + \ln(A_p) + \alpha \ln(\hat{L}_p) + \beta \ln(\hat{K}_p) + \gamma \ln(\hat{I}_p)$$

By inverting this equation, employment can be expressed as a function of the other variables, including sales. Adding the subscripts $t$for a given year, as well as (i) year fixed-effects, δ_t, to account for common macroeconomic shocks across industries; (ii) industry fixed-effects, δ_p, to account for the level of mark-up – which depends on competition within the industry, the price elasticity of demand, etc.; and the TFP, which may be considered as constant in the short run (i.e. in the case of this study, three years) – the following econometric specification is obtained:

$$\ln(\hat{L}_{pt}) = \beta_0 + \delta_t + \delta_p + \beta_1 \ln(\hat{K}_{pt}) + \beta_2 \ln(\hat{I}_{pt}) + \beta_3 \ln(\hat{S}_{pt}) + \sum\nolimits_p \beta_p [\ln(\hat{S}_{pt}) \times \delta_p] + \varepsilon_{pt}$$

with β_0 a constant and ε_{pt} the error term. The estimates of the elasticity of employment with respect to sales for each industry can then be extracted from the equation above, and are given by $\xi_p = \beta_3 + \beta_p$. An estimated elasticity of ξ_p means that a decrease of 1% in sales translates into a decrease of ξ_p% in jobs.

The results of the econometric specification summarized by the last equation for the Italian retail and wholesale sector are displayed in Table A.1. The first column shows the coefficients estimated without the inclusion of industry fixed-effects, and indicates an increase of 1% in sales in the retail and wholesale sector implies on average a 0.37% increase in the number of employees within the sector. The second column of Table A.1 adds cross-effects between the logarithm of sales and the industry fixed-effects to the econometric specification, which leads to the industry-specific estimates of the elasticity of employment with respect to sales displayed below.

Table A.1. Estimations of sales elasticity of employment, Italian wholesale and retail sector

Dependent variable: log employment		
log Capital	0.019**	0.020***
	(0.008)	(0.008)
log Intermediate inputs	-0.278*	-0.216*
	(0.155)	(-0.071)
log Productivity	-0.095**	-0.101**
	(-0.019)	(-0.023)
log Wages	-0.467***	-0.460***
	(0.103)	(0.098)
log Sales	0.410***	0.420***
	(0.107)	(0.096)
constant	5.531***	5.615***
	(0.264)	(0.781)
Industry fixed-effects	Yes	Yes
Year fixed-effects	Yes	Yes
Cross log Sales x Industry fixed-effects	No	Yes
Adjusted R2	0.883	0.888
Number of observations	72	72

Notes: Standard errors in parentheses. * p<0.10; ** p<0.05; *** p<0.01. The industrial data for Italian industries over the period 2008-15 are provided by Eurostat Eurostat (2018). Employment is measured by the number of full-time equivalent employees; capital by the gross investment in intangible goods; intermediate inputs by total purchases of goods and services; sales by turnovers; wages by the ratio of total personal costs.

The estimates of the sales elasticity of employment for each category of the Italian retail and wholesale industry are reported in Table A.2. Clearly, a decrease in sales does not translate into the same proportion of lost jobs in each sector. For instance, while a decline of 1% in sales for the Italian wholesale and retail sector of watches and jewellery induces a 0.35% decline in the number of employees within this sector, the elasticity is far higher for the wholesale and retail sector of food, beverage and tobacco, with an estimated transmission rate of 0.42%.

Table A.2. Elasticity of employment with respect to sales in the Italian wholesale and retail sector

Estimates for 2011-2013

Sector	Sales elasticity of employment (ε_p)
Food, beverages and tobacco	0.419
Mineral products (e.g. fuels, ores)	0.377
Chemical and allied products; except pharmaceuticals, perfumery and cosmetics	0.348
Pharmaceutical and medicinal chemical products	0.373
Perfumery and cosmetics	0.392
Textiles and other intermediate products (e.g. plastics; rubbers; paper; wood)	0.391
Clothing, footwear, leather and related products	0.400
Watches and jewellery	0.355
Non-metallic mineral products (e.g. glass and glass products, ceramic products)	0.390
Basic metals and fabricated metal products (except machinery and equipment)	0.384
Electrical household appliances, electronic and telecommunications equipment	0.371
Machinery, industrial equipment; computers and peripheral equipment; ships and aircrafts	0.377
Motor vehicles and motorcycles	0.405
Household cultural and recreation goods; including toys and games, books and musical instruments	0.365
Furniture, lighting equipment, carpets and other manufacturing n.e.c	0.396

Estimates of job losses

Once estimated, these transmission rates between sales and jobs can be used to estimate the share of lost jobs due to counterfeit products smuggled into Italy in total employment. For each Italian retail and wholesale sector, this is done by multiplying the transmission rate with the share of lost sales by the total sales of genuine products. Finally, applying these shares of lost jobs onto data on the level of employment in a given sector makes it possible to estimate the number of jobs lost in the Italian wholesale and retail industry due to counterfeit products smuggled into Italy.

More formally, the estimated transmission rates between sales and jobs, ε_p, allow recovering the number of lost jobs as follows. First, the share of lost jobs due to counterfeit and pirated imports into the total employment within each retail and wholesale industry, ϑ_p, is calculated by multiplying the share of lost sales into the total sales of genuine products in the industry, $S_p/\hat{S}_p$, with the transmission rates:

$$\vartheta_p = \varepsilon_p \times \left(S_p/\hat{S}_p\right)$$

Second, these shares of lost jobs are applied onto data on the level of employment, $\hat{L}_p$. This give us the amount of lost jobs in the wholesale and retail industries due to counterfeit and pirated imports, J_p:

$$J_p = \vartheta_p \times \hat{L}_p$$

Step 6: Determining taxes forgone

Lower genuine sales due to counterfeit and pirated imports reduce several sources of revenue for the Italian Government:

- value-added taxes (VAT) that would have been collected on consumption at purchase.

- corporate income taxes (CIT) that would have been collected from firms in the wholesale and retail industry.
- social security contributions (SSC) from employees and employers in the retail and wholesale industry.
- personal income taxes (PIT) from employees and employers in the retail and wholesale industry.

In order to calculate the lost VAT, one simply needs to apply the VAT rates on the amount of total lost sales due to counterfeit and pirated imports estimated in Step 4.

The amount of government taxes lost from CIT is calculated by multiplying the average profit rates within each category of retail and wholesale industry by the average rate of corporation tax taking into account the estimated value of lost sales.

To calculate losses in social security contributions, the share of the actual average amount of SSC paid by employees and employers for one unit of employment is multiplied by the amount of estimated lost jobs due to counterfeit and pirated imports estimated in Step 5.

The PIT foregone is calculated by multiplying the average salary in a given industry by the average income tax rate times the amount of lost jobs.

Note that in order to estimate the results as accurately as possible, these four types of lost revenues were calculated by industry. The final result at the national level was obtained by adding the estimated amounts of forgone tax revenues across industries.

A.3. Gauging the direct effects of trade in fake goods that infringe Italian trademarks and patents

There are three ways through which global trade in goods infringing Italian trademarks and patents can affect the Italian economy: 1) loss of sales for IPR owners; 2) job losses in the manufacturing sector; 3) forgone tax revenues for the Italian Government. These can be calculated using a harmonised methodology that follows a number of steps:

- Step 7: Evaluation of the worldwide volume of infringement of Italian IP rights holders
- Step 8: Market analysis of residents' IPR-infringing goods sold worldwide (primary/secondary)
- Step 9: Analysis of lost sales for IP right holders
- Step 10: Estimation of lost jobs for manufacturing industries
- Step 11: Estimation of forgone taxes.

All these steps are presented in Figure A.3 and described in detail in the paragraphs that follow.

Importantly, all other impact areas are hard to measure quantitatively, or are likely to occur in the long term, and are therefore excluded from the analysis.

Figure A.3. Analysis of the direct effects on Italian IPR holders of global trade in fakes

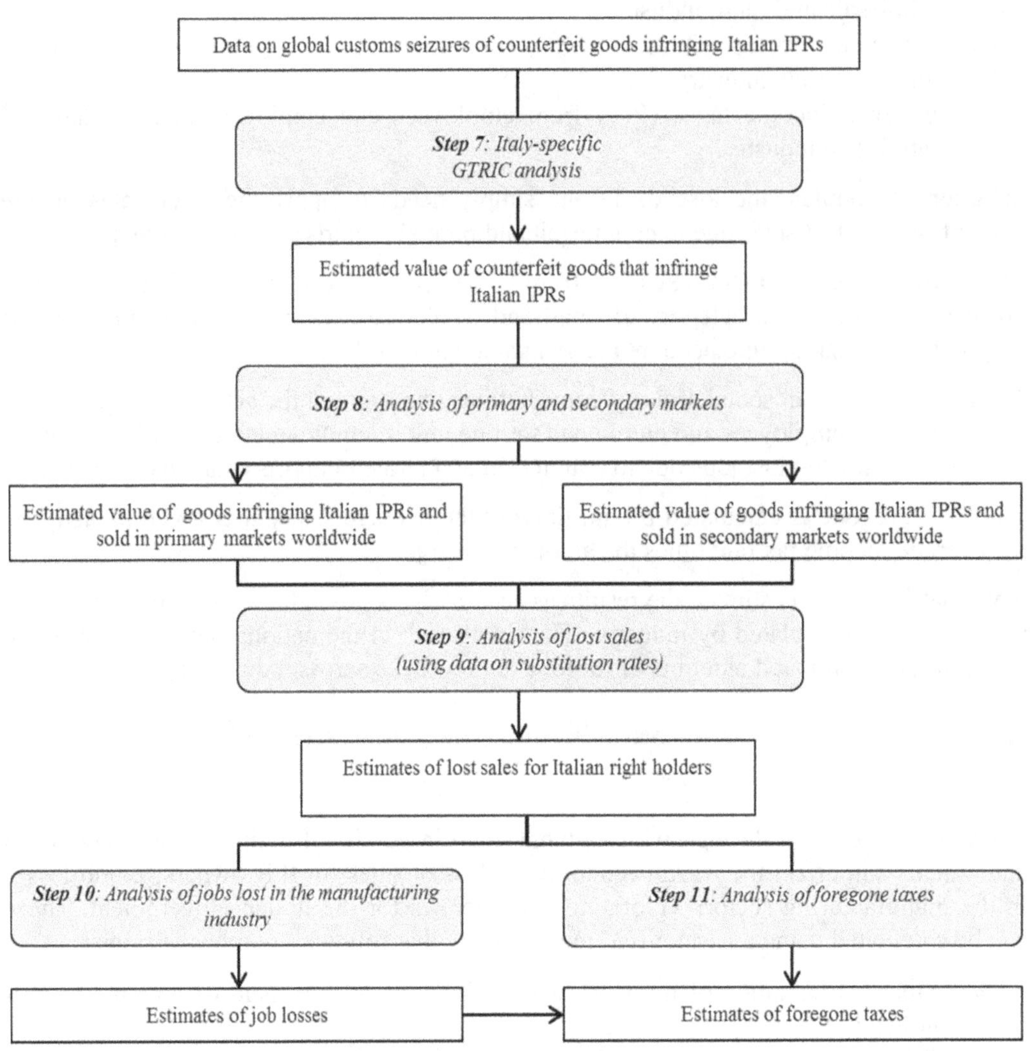

Step 7: Evaluating the worldwide volume of infringements of IPRs on Italian rights holders.

The first step is to estimate the value of counterfeit goods traded worldwide that infringe trademarks or patents held by Italian rights owners. For this purpose, observations in the database that refer to trademarks or patents whose rights holders' address is registered in Italy were selected. Note that the identification of rights holders' locations was done using the Global Brand Database WIPO (2016) and the PATENTSCOPE database WIPO (2017), both provided by the World Intellectual Property Organisation.

From this data selection, the value of global counterfeiting targeting the IPR of Italian residents can be assessed by product category and destination economy, by adapting the GTRIC methodology developed in OECD/EUIPO (2016) for exports and domestic sales.

The indices included in the GTRIC matrix refer to the likelihood that a given type of counterfeit product of a brand or patent whose rights holder's location is registered in Italy is sold in a given destination economy, including Italy. These indices are then applied to existing statistics on exports and domestic sales to estimate the overall magnitude of global trade in counterfeit and pirated products that infringe Italian residents' IPR.

This methodology allows the general exporting and selling behaviour of industries to be taken into account, and relies on three key econometric components:

- The General Trade-Related Index of Counterfeiting for economies (GTRIC-e) – an index that lists economies according to their proneness to be a destination for counterfeit and pirated products of brands registered in Italy (Step 7)
- The General Trade-Related Index of Counterfeiting for Italian products (GTRIC-p) – an index that lists Italian industries according to their proneness to sell products that are sensitive to global counterfeiting and piracy (Step 8)
- The general matrix (GTRIC) that compares the likelihood of products sold by a given industry in a given destination economy to be counterfeit or pirated with the most sensitive "product category-destination economy" pair (Step 9).

Applying the GTRIC matrix to data on exports and domestic sales allows the "ceiling" value to be gauged for trade in counterfeit and pirated goods infringing the IPR owned by Italian residents. One issue, however, is how to establish a fixed point, i.e. an upper limit of counterfeit trade in percentage of exports, for the "product category–destination economy" pairs most sensitive to global counterfeiting and piracy.

Since the interviews with customs officials and experts could not determine these fixed points, the empirical application is based on three scenarios, with selected values of 10%, 15% and 20%. Note that all of these scenarios take much more conservative values of fixed points than the actual fixed points applied to imports in OECD-EUIPO (2016).

These fixed points, when combined with the relative likelihood included in the GTRIC matrix, enable calculation of the share of exports and, importantly, of domestic sales of products infringing residents' IPRs. Applying these shares to statistics on the value of exports and domestic sales gives the estimated value of goods infringing residents' IPR by product category and destination economy.

Step 8: Market analysis of fake goods infringing Italian IPRs

As with the previous analysis, two issues now need to be addressed in order to assess the economic impact of infringements of domestic rights owners' trademarks and patents in global trade. First, what share of these counterfeit products is traded on primary versus secondary markets worldwide? Second, within secondary markets, what is the rate at which consumers across the world would have substituted counterfeit goods for their legitimate copies?

The first issue is addressed with the exact same methodology as described in the first part of Step 2. The only slight difference is that the unit value distributions are estimated for each "product category - trademark (or patent) - destination economy" triplet, in order to take into account differences in retail prices between economies.

For example, between 2011 and 2013, the most counterfeited "Italian" products were the Ray-Ban sunglasses produced by the Italian eyewear conglomerate Luxottica Group. The OECD database on global customs seizures includes almost 5 600 customs seizures of this product recorded in 64 destination economies. Figure A.4 shows the unit value distribution of those fake sunglasses seized worldwide. Using the methodology outlined indicates that fake Ray-Ban sunglasses with prices lower than 120 euros were destined for the secondary market, while those with values higher than 120 euros (the peaks on the right hand side of the distribution) were targeted at the primary market.

Figure A.4. Price distribution of counterfeit Ray-Ban sunglasses seized worldwide, 2011-2013

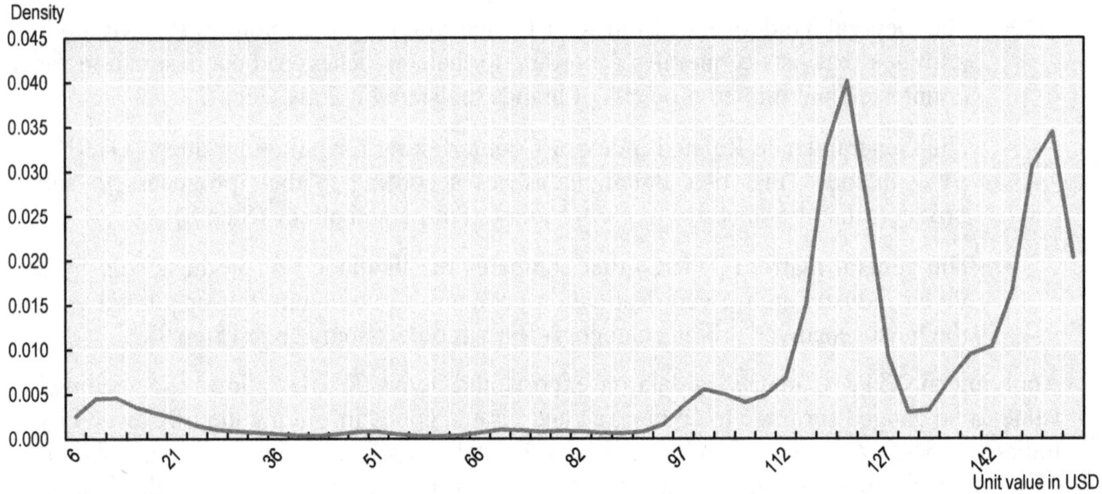

Finally, because of a lack of data, the consumers' substitution rates chosen are the same as those selected in the second part of Step 2. Again, different scenarios of lost sales, lost jobs and lost taxes will be presented depending on the assumed rates.

Step 9. Estimating lost sales for Italian IPR owners

In order to discover the value of lost sales for Italian IPR owners, the estimated value of products sold worldwide that are fake versions of these brands or patents are **combined** with information on 1) the share of primary and secondary markets for these products by destination economy; and 2) consumers' substitution rates (see Step 8).

The calculation is very close to the one described in Step 4, the only exception being that it is first performed by destination economy before being aggregated. The total value of lost sales for domestic rights owners is given by adding the value of sales of fake products on primary markets to the value of sales on the secondary market, adjusted for consumers' substitution rates.

Formally, by denoting τ_{pd}^{1} the share of the primary market in destination economy d for all products of type p that infringe residents' IPR, and C_{pd} the estimated value of fake sales of those products in that destination, the estimated value of lost sales for domestic right holders by product category p is given by:

$$S_p = \sum_d \left[\tau_{pd}^{1} \times C_{pd}\right] + \left[(1 - \tau_{pd}^{1}) \times C_{pd} \times \rho_p\right]$$

with ρ_p denoting the product type-specific consumers' substitution rates.

Step 10: Estimating job losses in the Italian manufacturing sector

This step requires estimating the extent to which employment in the Italian manufacturing sector responds to changes in sales on export markets and on the domestic market. This is done by applying the econometric model developed in Step 5 to data specific to the manufacturing industries.

The results of this estimation for the Italian manufacturing sector are displayed in Table A.3. The main insight at the aggregate level is that an increase of 1% in sales in the Italian manufacturing sector implies on average a 0.51% increase in the number of employees within the sector.

Table A.3. Estimation of sales elasticity of employment, Italian manufacturing sector

Dependent variable: log employment		
log Capital	0.021*	0.023*
	(0.009)	(0.012)
log Intermediate Inputs	-0.416*	-0.556*
	(0.181)	(0.221)
log Productivity	-0.295***	-0.241***
	(0.044)	(0.057)
log Wages	-0.614***	-0.596***
	(0.108)	(0.128)
log Sales	0.513***	0.612***
	(0.141)	(0.193)
constant	-1.712**	-1.867**
	(0.612)	(0.639)
Industry fixed-effects	Yes	Yes
Year fixed-effects	Yes	Yes
Cross log Sales x Industry fixed-effects	No	Yes
Adjusted R^2	0.905	0.907
Number of observations	55	55

Notes: Standard errors in parentheses. * p<0.05; ** p<0.01; *** p<0.001. The industrial data for Italian industries over the period 2011-13 are provided by Eurostat (2018). Employment is measured by the number of full-time equivalent employees; capital by the gross investment in intangible goods; intermediate inputs by total purchases of goods and services; sales by turnovers; wages by the ratio of total personal costs, including social security costs, to the number of full-time equivalent employees; productivity by labour productivity.

The estimates of the sales elasticity of employment for each Italian manufacturing industry are reported in Table A.4. Again, a decrease in sales does not translate into the same proportion of lost jobs in each one of them. For instance, while a decline of 1% in sales for the industry of pharmaceuticals and medicinal chemical products induces a 0.7285% decline in the number of employees within this sector, the transmission rate is far lower for the building of machinery and industrial equipment, with an estimated transmission rate of 0.43%.

Table A.4. Elasticity of employment with respect to sales in the Italian manufacturing sector

Estimates for 2011-2013

Sector	Sales elasticity of employment (ε_p)
Food, beverages and tobacco	0.593
Mineral products (e.g. fuels, ores)	0.507
Chemical and allied products; except pharmaceuticals, perfumery and cosmetics	0.483
Pharmaceutical and medicinal chemical products	0.720
Perfumery and cosmetics	0.524
Textiles and other intermediate products (e.g. plastics; rubbers; paper; wood)	0.634
Clothing, footwear, leather and related products	0.638
Watches and jewellery	0.484
Non-metallic mineral products (e.g. glass and glass products, ceramic products)	0.667
Basic metals and fabricated metal products (except machinery and equipment)	0.520
Electrical household appliances, electronic and telecommunications equipment	0.457
Machinery, industrial equipment; computers and peripheral equipment; ships and aircrafts	0.432
Motor vehicles and motorcycles	0.451
Household cultural and recreation goods; including toys and games, books and musical instruments	0.534
Furniture, lighting equipment, carpets and other manufacturing n.e.c	0.432

Once estimated, these transmission rates between sales and jobs can be used to estimate the share of lost jobs due to infringements in global trade of Italian trademarks and patents in total employment. For each Italian manufacturing industry, this is done by multiplying the transmission rate with the share of lost sales for Italian IPR owners. Finally, multiplying these shares of lost jobs onto data on the level of employment within each manufacturing industry makes it possible to estimate the number of jobs lost in Italian manufacturing industries lost due to infringements of Italian IPR in global trade.

More formally, the estimated transmission rates between sales and jobs,ε_p, allow recovering the number of lost jobs as follows. First, the share of lost jobs due to infringements in global trade of Italian trademarks and patents into the total employment within each manufacturing industry, ϑ_p, is calculated by multiplying the share of lost sales into the total sales of genuine products in the industry, $S_p/\hat{S}_p$, with the transmission rates.

Step 11: Determining forgone tax revenues

Jobs lost due to infringements of IPRs, unlike those lost due to counterfeit and pirated imports, affect only three types of tax revenues: corporate income taxes of rights holders; social security contributions; and personal income taxes paid by employers and employees in the manufacturing sector. The value-added taxes on domestic sales of Italian IPR-infringing products are not calculated, since they have already been taken into account when estimating the value of forgone tax revenues induced by lost sales due to counterfeit and pirated imports.

The methodologies applied to calculate each of these forgone tax revenues are exactly the same as those described in Step 6. Again, this is done industry by industry in order to obtain estimates as accurate as possible.

A.4. Construction of the GTRIC for the counterfeit market in Italy

Construction of GTRIC-p

GTRIC-p is constructed in three steps:

1. For each product category, the seizure percentages for sensitive goods are formed.
2. From these, a counterfeit source factor is established for each industry, based on the industries' weight in terms of Italian imports.
3. Based on these factors, the GTRIC-p is formed.

Step 1: Measuring product seizure frequencies

v_p and m_p are, respectively, the seizure and import values of product type p (as registered according to the HS on the two-digit level) sold in Italy from *any* provenance economy in a given year. The relative seizure frequencies (seizure percentages) of good p, denoted below by γ_p, is then defined by:

$$\gamma_p = \frac{v_p}{\sum_p v_p}, \text{ such that } \sum\nolimits_p \gamma_p = 1$$

Step 2: Measuring industry -specific counterfeiting factors

$M = \sum_p m_p$ is defined as the total registered imports of all sensitive goods in Italy.

The share of good p in Italian imports, denoted by s_p, is therefore given by:

$$s_p = \frac{m_p}{M}, \text{ such that } \sum\nolimits_p s_p = 1$$

The counterfeiting factor of product category p, denoted by C_p, is then determined as the following.

$$C_p = \frac{\gamma_p}{s_p}$$

The counterfeiting factor reflects the sensitivity of product infringements occurring in a particular product category, relative to its share in Italian imports. These constitute the foundation for forming GTRIC-p.

Step 3: Establishing GTRIC-p

GTRIC-p is constructed from a transformation of the counterfeiting factor; it measures the relative likelihood of different types of product categories being subject to counterfeiting and piracy in Italian imports. The transformation of the counterfeiting factor is based on two main assumptions:

1. The first (A1) is that the counterfeiting factor of a particular product category is positively correlated with the actual degree of trade in counterfeit and pirated goods covered by that chapter. The counterfeiting factors must thus reflect the real intensity of actual counterfeit trade in the given product categories.
2. The second (A2) acknowledges that the assumption A1 may not be entirely correct. For instance, the fact infringing goods are detected more frequently in certain categories could imply differences in counterfeiting factors across products merely reflect that some goods are easier to detect than others, or that some goods, for one reason or another, have been specially targeted for inspection. The counterfeiting

factors of product categories with lower counterfeiting factors could therefore underestimate actual counterfeiting and piracy intensities in these cases.

In accordance with assumption A1 (positive correlation between counterfeiting factors and actual infringement activities) and assumption A2 (lower counterfeiting factors may underestimate actual activities), GTRIC-p is established by applying a positive monotonic transformation of the counterfeiting factor index using natural logarithms. This standard technique of linearisation of a non-linear relationship (in the case of this study, between counterfeiting factors and actual infringement activities) allows the index to be flattened and gives a higher relative weight to lower counterfeiting factors Verbeek (2008).

In order to address the possibility of outliers at both ends of the counterfeiting factor index – i.e. some categories may be measured as particularly susceptible to infringement even though they are not, whereas others may be measured as unsusceptible although they are – it is assumed that GTRIC-p follows a left-truncated normal distribution, with GTRIC-p only taking values of zero or above.

The transformed counterfeiting factor is defined as:

$$c_p = \ln(C_p + 1)$$

Assuming the transformed counterfeiting factor can be described by a left-truncated normal distribution with $c_p \geq 0$; then, following Hald (1952), the density function of GTRIC-p is given by:

$$f_{LTN}(c_p) = \begin{cases} 0 & if\, c_p \leq 0 \\ \dfrac{f(c_p)}{\int_0^{\infty} f(c_p)\, dc_p} & if\, c_p \geq 0 \end{cases}$$

where $f(c_p)$ is the non-truncated normal distribution for c_p , specified as:

$$f(c_p) = \frac{1}{\sqrt{2\pi\sigma_p^2}} \exp\left(-\frac{1}{2}\left(\frac{c_p - \mu_p}{\sigma_p}\right)^2\right)$$

The mean and variance of the normal distribution, here denoted by μ_p and σ_p^2 , are estimated over the transformed counterfeiting factor index, c_p, and given by $\hat{\mu}_p$ and $\hat{\sigma}_p^2$. This enables the calculation of the counterfeit import proneness index (GTRIC-p) across product categories, corresponding to the cumulative distribution function of c_p.

Construction of GTRIC-e

GTRIC-e is also constructed in three steps:

1. For each provenance economy, the seizure percentages are calculated.
2. From these, each provenance economy's counterfeit source factor is established, based on the provenance economies' weight in terms of Italian total imports.
3. Based on these factors, the GTRIC-e is formed.

Step 1: Measuring seizure intensities from each provenance economy

v_e is Italy's registered seizures of all types of infringing goods (i.e. all p) originating from economy e during a given year in terms of their value.

γ_e is Italy's relative seizure frequency (seizure percentage) of all infringing items that originate from economy e, in a given year:

$$\gamma_e = \frac{v_e}{\sum_e v_e}, \text{ such that } \sum_e \gamma_e = 1$$

Step 2: Measuring economy-specific counterfeiting factors

m_e is defined as the total registered Italian imports of all sensitive products from e, and $M = \sum_e m_e$ is the total Italian import of sensitive goods from all provenance economies.

The share of imports from provenance economy e in total Italian imports of sensitive goods, denoted by s_e, is then given by:

$$s_e = \frac{m_e}{M}, \text{ such that } \sum_e s_e = 1$$

From this, the economy-specific counterfeiting factor is established by dividing the general seizure frequency for economy e with the share of total imports of sensitive goods from e.

$$C_e = \frac{\gamma_e}{s_e}$$

Step 3: Establishing GTRIC-e

Gauging the magnitude of counterfeiting and piracy from a provenance economy perspective can be undertaken in a fashion similar to that for sensitive goods. Hence, a general trade-related index of counterfeiting for economies (GTRIC-e) is established along similar lines and assumptions:

1. The first assumption (A3) is that the frequency with which any counterfeit or pirated article from a particular economy is detected and seized by customs is positively correlated with the actual amount of counterfeit and pirate articles imported from that location.

2. The second assumption (A4) acknowledges that assumption A3 may not be entirely correct. For instance, a high seizure intensity of counterfeit or pirated articles from a particular provenance economy could be an indication that the provenance economy is part of a customs profiling scheme, or that it is specially targeted for investigation by customs. The role that provenance economies with low seizure intensities play regarding actual counterfeiting and piracy activity could therefore be underrepresented by the index and lead to an underestimation of the scale of counterfeiting and piracy.

As with the product-specific index, GTRIC-e is established by applying a positive monotonic transformation of the counterfeiting factor index for provenance economies using natural logarithms. This follows from assumption A3 (positive correlation between seizure intensities and actual infringement activities) and assumption A4 (lower intensities tend to underestimate actual activities). Considering the possibilities of outliers at both ends of the GTRIC-e distribution – i.e. some economies may be wrongly measured as being particularly susceptible sources of counterfeit and pirated imports, and vice versa – GTRIC-e is approximated by a left-truncated normal distribution as it does not take values below zero.

The transformed general counterfeiting factor across provenance economies on which GTRIC-e is based is therefore given by applying logarithms onto economy-specific general counterfeit factors Verbeek (2008):

$$c_e = \ln(C_e + 1)$$

In addition, following GTRIC-p it is assumed that GTRIC-e follows a truncated normal distribution with $c_e \geq 0$ for all e. Following Hald (1952), the density function of the left-truncated normal distribution for c_e is given by

$$g_{LTN}(c_p) = \begin{cases} 0 & if cf_e \leq 0 \\ \dfrac{g(e)}{\int_0^{\infty} g(c_e)\, dc_e} & if cf_e \geq 0 \end{cases}$$

where $g(c_e)$ is the non-truncated normal distribution for c_e , specified as:

$$g(c_e) = \frac{1}{\sqrt{2\pi\sigma_e^2}} \exp\left(-\frac{1}{2}\left(\frac{c_e - \mu_e}{\sigma_e}\right)^2\right)$$

The mean and variance of the normal distribution, here denoted by μ_e and σ_e^2, are estimated over the transformed counterfeiting factor index, c_e, and given by $\hat{\mu}_e$ and $\hat{\sigma}_e^2$. This enables the calculation of the counterfeit import propensity index (GTRIC-e) across provenance economies, corresponding to the cumulative distribution function ofc_e.

Construction of GTRIC

The combined index of GTRIC-e and GTRIC-p, denoted by GTRIC, is an index that approximates the relative proneness of particular product types, imported by Italy from specific trading partners, to be counterfeit and/or pirated.

Step 1: Establishing intensities for products and provenance economies

In this step the proneness to contain counterfeit and pirated products will be established for each trade flow from a given provenance economy and in a given product category.

The general proneness of product category p to be infringed, from any economy, is denoted by P_p and given by GTRIC-p so that:

$$P_p = F_{LTN}(c_p)$$

where $F_{LTN}(c_p)$ is the cumulative probability function of $f_{LTN}(c_p)$.

Furthermore, the general propensity of infringing goods of any type from economy e is denoted by P_e, and given by GTRIC-e, so that:

$$P_e = G_{LTN}(c_e)$$

where $G_{LTN}(c_e)$ is the cumulative probability function of $g_{LTN}(c_e)$.

The general likelihood of items of type p originating from economy e to be counterfeit or pirated is then denoted by P_{ep} and approximated by:

$$P_{ep} = P_p P_e$$

Therefore, $P_{ep} \in [\varepsilon_p \varepsilon_e \,; 1]$, $\forall e, p$, with $\varepsilon_p \varepsilon_e$ denoting the minimum average counterfeit export rate for each sensitive product category and each provenance economy. It is assumed that $\varepsilon_e = \varepsilon_p = 0.05$.

Step 2: Calculating the absolute value

α is the fixed point, i.e. the maximum average counterfeit rate of a given type of infringing good, p, originating from a given economy e. α can therefore be applied onto likelihood of goods of type p from trading partner e to be infringed (αP^{jk}).

As a result, a matrix of counterfeit proneness C is obtained.

$$C = \begin{pmatrix} \alpha P_{11} & \alpha P_{12} & & & \alpha P_{1P} \\ \alpha P_{21} & \ddots & & & \\ & & \alpha P_{ep} & & \\ & & & \ddots & \\ \alpha P_{E1} & & & & \alpha P_{EP} \end{pmatrix} \text{ with dimension } E \times P$$

The matrix of Italian imports is denoted by M. Applying C on M yields the absolute volume of counterfeit and pirated imports in the Italy. In particular, the imports matrix M is given by:

$$M = \begin{pmatrix} m_{11} & m_{12} & & & m_{1P} \\ m_{21} & \ddots & & & \\ & & m_{ep} & & \\ & & & \ddots & \\ m_{E1} & & & & m_{EP} \end{pmatrix} \text{ with dimension } E \times P$$

Hence, the element m_{ep} denotes Italian imports of product category p from partner e, with $e = [1, \dots, E]$ and $p = [1, \dots, P]$.

Denoted by Ψ, the product-by-economy percentage of counterfeit and pirated imports can be determined as the following:

$$\Psi = \mathrm{C'M} \div \mathrm{M}$$

The value of total imports of counterfeit and pirated goods, denoted by the scalar TC, is then given by:

$$\mathrm{TC} = \mathrm{I}_1' \Psi \mathrm{I}_2$$

where I_1 is an identity matrix with dimension $E \times 1$, and I_2 is an identity matrix with dimension $P \times 1$.

By denoting total world trade by the scalar $\mathrm{TM} = \mathrm{I}_1 \mathrm{M}' \mathrm{I}_2$, the share of imports of counterfeit and pirated products into total Italian imports, S_{TC}, is determined by:

$$S_{TC} = \frac{TC}{TM}$$

A.5. Construction of the GTRIC for products infringing Italian IPR

Construction of Italian GTRIC-p

Italian GTRIC-p is constructed in three steps:

- For each product category, the seizure percentages for sensitive goods are formed.
- From these, a counterfeit source factor is established for each industry, based on the industries' weight in terms of total trade.
- Based on these factors, the GTRIC-p is formed.

Step 1: Measuring product seizure frequencies

w_q is the seized value of product type q infringing Italian residents' IPR from *any* provenance economy in a given year. The relative seizure frequency (seizure percentages) of good q, denoted below as η_q, is then defined by:

$$\eta_q = \frac{w_q}{\sum_q w_q}, \quad \text{such that} \sum_q \eta_q = 1$$

Step 2: Measuring product-specific counterfeiting factors

e_q is the global sales value (exports plus domestic sales) of all Italian branded products of type q, so that $E = \sum_q e_q$ is defined as the global registered sales by Italian manufacturing industries of *all* sensitive goods.

The share of good q in Italian total sales, denoted by ς_q, is therefore given by:

$$\varsigma_q = \frac{e_q}{E}, \quad \text{such that} \sum_q \varsigma_q = 1$$

The counterfeiting factor of product category q, denoted C_q, is then determined as the following.

$$C_q = \frac{\eta_q}{\varsigma_q}$$

The counterfeiting factor reflects the sensitivity of infringements of Italian trademarks and patents occurring in a particular product category, relative to its share in Italian global sales. These constitute the foundation for forming GTRIC-p.

Step 3: Establishing Italian GTRIC-p

GTRIC-p is constructed from a transformation of the counterfeiting factor; it measures the relative proneness with which Italian trademarks and patents in different types of product categories are subject to counterfeiting and piracy. The transformation of the counterfeiting factor is based on two main assumptions, described in OECD/EUIPO (2016):

1. The first (A5) is that the counterfeiting factor for goods infringing Italian IPR of a particular product category is positively correlated with the actual degree of trade in counterfeit and pirated goods covered by that chapter. The counterfeiting factors must thus reflect the real intensity of actual counterfeit trade for products infringing Italian IPR in the given product categories.

2. The second (A6) acknowledges that the assumption A5 may not be entirely correct. For instance, the fact Italian IPR infringing goods are detected more frequently in certain categories could imply that differences in counterfeiting factors across products merely reflect that some goods infringing Italian IPR are easier to detect than others, or that some of these goods, for one reason or another, have been specially targeted by customs worldwide. The counterfeiting factors of product categories with lower counterfeiting factors could therefore underestimate actual counterfeiting and piracy intensities in these cases.

In accordance with assumptions A5 and A6, GTRIC-p for products infringing Italian IPR traded worldwide is established by applying a positive monotonic transformation of the counterfeiting factor index using natural logarithms. This standard technique of linearisation of a non-linear relationship – in the case of this study between counterfeiting factors and actual infringement activities – allows the index to be flattened and gives a higher relative weight to lower counterfeiting factors Verbeek (2008).

In addition, in order to address the possibility of outliers at both ends of the counterfeiting factor index – i.e. some categories may be measured as particularly susceptible to infringement even though they are not, whereas others may be measured as unsusceptible although they are – it is assumed that GTRIC-p follows a left-truncated normal distribution, with GTRIC-p only taking values of zero or above.

The transformed counterfeiting factor is defined as:

$$c_q = \ln(C_q + 1)$$

Assuming that the transformed counterfeiting factor can be described by a left-truncated normal distribution with $c_k \geq 0$; then, following Hald (1952), the density function of GTRIC-p is given by:

$$h_{LTN}(c_q) = \begin{cases} 0 & if c_q \leq 0 \\ \dfrac{h(c_q)}{\int_0^{\infty} h(c_q)\, dc_q} & if c_q \geq 0 \end{cases}$$

where $h(c_q)$ is the non-truncated normal distribution for c_k, specified as:

$$h(c_q) = \frac{1}{\sqrt{2\pi\sigma_q^2}} \exp\left(-\frac{1}{2}\left(\frac{c_q - \mu_q}{\sigma_q}\right)^2\right)$$

The mean and variance of the normal distribution, here denoted by μ_q and σ_q^2 , are estimated over the transformed counterfeiting factor index, c_q, and given by $\hat{\mu}_q$ and $\hat{\sigma}_q^2$. This enables calculation of the counterfeit propensity index (GTRIC-p) across HS chapters, corresponding to the cumulative distribution function of c_q.

Construction of GTRIC-e

GTRIC-e is also constructed in three steps:

- For each provenance economy, the seizure percentages are calculated.
- From these, each provenance economy's counterfeit source factor is established, based on the provenance economies' weight in terms of Italian total sales.
- Based on these factors, the GTRIC-e is formed.

Step 1: Measuring seizure intensities for each destination economy

w_d is the registered seized value of all types of goods infringing Italian residents' IP rights (i.e. all q) exported to destination economy d from any provenance economy at a given year. η_d is the relative seizure intensity (seizure percentage) of all products infringing Italian trademarks and patents that are shipped to country d, in a given year:

$$\eta_d = \frac{w_d}{\sum_d w_d}, \text{ such that } \sum\nolimits_d \eta_d = 1$$

Step 2: Measuring destination-specific counterfeiting factors

e_d is defined as the global registered sales value of Italian branded or patented products (exports plus domestic manufacturing sales) shipped to d (including Italy) and $E = \sum_d e_d$ is the global value of Italian sales of sensitive goods to all destination economies.

The share of sales to destination economy d in Italian global sales of sensitive goods, denoted ς_d, is then given by:

$$\varsigma_d = \frac{e_d}{E}, \text{ such that } \sum_d \varsigma_d = 1$$

From this, the economy-specific counterfeiting factor is established by dividing the seizure intensity for economy d by the share of total sales of sensitive goods to d:

$$C_d = \frac{\eta_d}{\varsigma_d}$$

Step 3: Establishing GTRIC-e

GTRIC-e is constructed from a transformation of the counterfeiting factor; it measures the relative proneness with which counterfeit products infringing Italian trademarks and patents are shipped to a given destination economy. The transformation of the counterfeiting factor is based on two main assumptions, described in OECD/EUIPO, (2016):

1. The first assumption (A7) is that the frequency with which any counterfeit Italian branded or patented article shipped to a particular destination economy is detected and seized by customs is positively correlated with the actual amount of counterfeit and pirated Italian products exported to that location; and
2. The second assumption (A8) acknowledges that assumption A7 may not be entirely correct. For instance, a high seizure intensity of products infringing Italian IPR in a particular destination economy could be an indication that the destination economy implements a particular customs profiling scheme, or that these products are specially targeted for investigation by customs in that locale. The role some destination economies with low seizure intensities of Italian IPR infringing products play regarding actual counterfeiting and piracy activity could therefore be underrepresented by the index and lead to an underestimation of the scale of counterfeiting activities and piracy targeting Italian branded or patented products there.

Following assumptions A7 and A8, GTRIC-e for products infringing Italian IPR is established by applying a positive monotonic transformation of the counterfeiting factor index using natural logarithms. This standard technique of linearisation of a non-linear relationship (in the case of this study, between counterfeiting factors and actual infringement activities) allows the index to be flattened and gives a higher relative weight to lower counterfeiting factors Verbeek (2008).

In addition, in order to address the possibility of outliers at both ends of the counterfeiting factor index – i.e. some destination economies may be measured as particularly susceptible to infringement even though they are not, whereas others may be measured as unsusceptible although they are – it is assumed GTRIC-e follows a left-truncated normal distribution, with GTRIC-e only taking values of zero or above.

The transformed general counterfeiting factor across destination economies on which GTRIC-e is based is therefore given by applying logarithms onto economy-specific general counterfeit factors Verbeek (2008):

$$c_d = \ln(C_d + 1)$$

In addition, following GTRIC-p it is assumed that GTRIC-e follows a truncated normal distribution with $c_d \geq 0$ for all d. Following Hald (1952)[24], the density function of the left-truncated normal distribution for c_d is given by

$$i_{LTN}(c_d) = \begin{cases} 0 & if\, c_d \leq 0 \\ \dfrac{i(c_d)}{\int_0^{\infty} i(c_d)\, dc_d} & if\, c_d \geq 0 \end{cases}$$

where $i(c_d)$ is the non-truncated normal distribution for c_d specified as:

$$i(c_d) = \frac{1}{\sqrt{2\pi\sigma_d^2}} \exp\left(-\frac{1}{2}\left(\frac{c_d - \mu_d}{\sigma_d}\right)^2\right)$$

The mean and variance of the normal distribution, here denoted by μ_d and σ_d^2, are estimated over the transformed counterfeiting factor index, c_d, and given by $\hat{\mu}_d$ and $\hat{\sigma}_d^2$. This enables the calculation of the counterfeit propensity index (GTRIC-e) across destination economies, corresponding to the cumulative distribution function of c_d.

Construction of GTRIC

The combined index of GTRIC-e and GTRIC-p, denoted GTRIC, is an index that approximates the relative proneness for goods associated with Italian residents' IP rights in a given product category and a given destination economy to be counterfeit and/or pirated.

Step 1: Establishing proneness for products and destination economies

The general proneness of Italian trademarks and patents to be counterfeit or pirated in product category q, is denoted by P_q, and is given by GTRIC-p, so that:

$$P_q = H_{LTN}(c_q)$$

where $H_{LTN}(c_q)$ is the cumulative probability function of $h_{LTN}(c_q)$.

Furthermore, the general proneness of all Italian trademarks and patents to be infringed and shipped to economy d is denoted by P_d, and is given by GTRIC-e, so that:

$$P_d = I_{LTN}(c_d)$$

where $I_{LTN}(c_d)$ is the cumulative probability function of $i_{LTN}(c_d)$

The general proneness of Italian residents' IP rights to be counterfeit or pirated in a given product category q and to be shipped to a given destination d from any provenance economy is then denoted by P_{kd} and approximated by:

$$P_{qd} = P_q \times P_d$$

Therefore, $P_{qd} \in [\varepsilon_q \varepsilon_d \,; 1]$, $\forall k, d$, with $\varepsilon_q \varepsilon_d$ denoting the minimum average counterfeit export rate for each sensitive product category and each destination economy. It is assumed that $\varepsilon_q = \varepsilon_d = 0.05$.

Step 2: Calculating the absolute value

β is the fixed point, i.e. the maximum average counterfeit rate of Italian trademarks and patents for a given product type q, shipped to a given trading partner, d. β can therefore be applied onto the proneness of Italian-related IP rights of type q to be counterfeit and shipped to destination partner d ($\beta \times P_{qd}$).

As a result, a matrix of counterfeit import propensities Λ is obtained.

$$\Lambda = \begin{pmatrix} \beta P_{11} & \beta P_{12} & & \beta P_{1Q} \\ \beta P_{21} & \ddots & & \\ & & \beta P_{dq} & \\ & & \ddots & \\ \beta P_{D1} & & & \beta P_{DQ} \end{pmatrix} \text{ with dimension } D \times Q$$

The matrix of Italian global sales is denoted by E. Applying Λ on E yields the absolute volume of counterfeit and pirated trade in products that infringe Italian residents' IPR. In particular, the sales matrix E is given by:

$$E = \begin{pmatrix} e_{11} & e_{12} & & e_{1Q} \\ e_{21} & \ddots & & \\ & & e_{dq} & \\ & & \ddots & \\ e_{D1} & & & e_{DQ} \end{pmatrix} \text{ with dimension } D \times Q$$

Hence, the element e_{dq} denotes Italian sales of products in category q to destination d, including Italy, with $d = [1, \dots, D]$ and $q = [1, \dots, Q]$.

Denoted by Z, the product-by-economy percentage of counterfeit and pirated imports can be determined as the following:

$$\mathrm{Z} = \Lambda'\mathrm{E} \div \mathrm{E}$$

Total trade in counterfeit and pirated goods that infringe Italian trademarks and patents, denoted by the scalar $\mathrm{T}\Lambda$, is then given by:

$$\mathrm{T}\Lambda = \mathrm{I}_1{}'\mathrm{Z}\mathrm{I}_2$$

where I_1 is an identity matrix with dimension $D \times 1$, and I_2 is an identity matrix with dimension $Q \times 1$.

Then, by denotingglobal Italian sales by the scalar $TE = I_1'ZE_2$, the share of counterfeit and pirated products infringing Italian residents' IPR in Italian global manufacturing sales, $\varsigma_{T\Lambda}$, is determined by:

$$\varsigma_{T\Lambda} = \frac{T\Lambda}{TE}$$

A.6. Sensitivity analysis

The sensitivity analysis is done to address the scarcity of data on substitution rates between fake and genuine goods. To carry out the analysis three different scenarios are introduced.

The first assumes substitution rates that follow the results of the Anti-Counterfeiting Group (2007) consumer survey and a survey carried out by Tom et al. (1998), the selected substitution rate is 32% for all other fake products sold on secondary markets. The second scenario is more conservative, and assumes substitution rates 10 percentage points lower. The third scenario is the most conservative one, and assumes the substitution rates to be 20 percentage points lower than in the first scenario. The three are recapped in Table A.5.

Table A.5. Assumed consumer substitution rates in the three performed scenarios

Sector	Scenario 1	Scenario 2	Scenario 3
Perfumery and cosmetics	49%	39%	29%
Watches and jewellery	27%	17%	7%
Clothing, accessories, leather and related products	39%	29%	19%
Other sectors	32%	22%	12%

Sources: Authors' own calculations based on Anti-Counterfeiting Group (2007) and Tom et al. (1998).

The three different scenarios are carried out independently to verify if the final result differ significantly, depending on changes in inputs. This is done for the following exercises:

- Estimation of lost sales for the Italian retail and wholesale sector (Table A.6).
- Estimation of lost jobs in the Italian retail and wholesale sector (Table A.7).
- Gauging of forgone taxes for the Italian government due to counterfeit and pirated imports (Table A.8)
- Estimation of lost sales for Italian manufacturing industries, (Table A.9)
- Estimation of lost jobs in Italian manufacturing industries(Table A.10)
- Calculation of public revenue losses due to Italian IPR infringements in global trade (Table A.11)

Importantly, in all cases the estimated losses for the three scenarios are very close, which confirms the robustness of all the results.

Table A.6. Sensitivity analysis: lost sales for the Italian retail and wholesale sector, 2013

Sector	Scenario 1		Scenario 2		Scenario 3	
	Value in EUR mn	Share of sales	Value in EUR mn	Share of sales	Value in EUR mn	Share of sales
Food, beverages and tobacco	618	1.0%	615	1.0%	612	1.0%
Chemical and allied products	125	3.7%	121	3.5%	117	3.4%
Pharmaceutical and medicinal chemical products	254	2.3%	245	2.2%	237	2.1%
Perfumery and cosmetics	85	1.6%	75	1.4%	65	1.2%
Textiles and other intermediate products	446	4.3%	411	3.9%	375	3.6%
Clothing, footwear, leather and related products	1269	4.4%	1163	4.0%	1056	3.7%
Watches and jewellery	221	7.5%	195	6.6%	169	5.8%
Non-metallic mineral products	16	0.2%	15	0.2%	13	0.2%
Basic metals and fabricated metal products	475	4.0%	471	4.0%	468	4.0%
Electronic and electrical equipment, optical products, scientific instruments	1794	5.4%	1611	4.9%	1427	4.3%
Machinery, industrial equipment; computers and peripheral equipment	732	4.1%	682	3.8%	631	3.5%
Motor vehicles and motorcycles	569	1.9%	502	1.7%	435	1.5%
Household cultural and recreation goods	212	2.1%	198	2.0%	185	1.9%
Furniturecarpets and other manufacturing n.e.c	132	0.6%	125	0.6%	118	0.6%
Total wholesale and resale sector	6949	2.7%	6429	2.4%	5909	2.2%

Table A.7. Sensitivity analysis: lost jobs in the Italian retail and wholesale sector, 2013

Sector	Scenario 1		Scenario 2		Scenario 3	
	Number	Share of jobs	Number	Share of jobs	Number	Share of jobs
Food, beverages and tobacco	3374	0.6%	3357	0.6%	3340	0.6%
Chemical and allied products	244	1.7%	235	1.7%	227	1.6%
Pharmaceutical and medicinal chemical products	565	1.2%	546	1.1%	527	1.1%
Perfumery and cosmetics	340	0.9%	301	0.8%	261	0.7%
Textiles and other intermediate products	1847	2.3%	1701	2.1%	1554	1.9%
Clothing, footwear, leather and related products	6582	2.4%	6029	2.2%	5476	2.0%
Watches and jewellery	797	3.6%	703	3.2%	609	2.8%
Non-metallic mineral products	65	0.1%	60	0.1%	55	0.1%
Basic metals and fabricated metal products	1649	2.1%	1635	2.1%	1622	2.1%
Electronic electrical and optical products, scientific instruments	1712	2.7%	1536	2.5%	1361	2.2%
Machinery, industrial equipment; computers and peripheral equipment	2262	2.1%	2106	1.9%	1950	1.8%
Motor vehicles and motorcycles	2272	1.1%	2005	0.9%	1738	0.8%
Household cultural and recreation goods	813	1.1%	762	1.0%	711	0.9%
Furniture, and other manufacturing n.e.c	629	0.3%	596	0.3%	564	0.3%
Total wholesale and retail sector	23149	1.3%	21573	1.2%	19997	1.1%

Table A.8. Sensitivity analysis: public revenue losses due to the fake imports in Italy, 2013

Tax type	Scenario 1		Scenario 2		Scenario 3	
	Value in EUR mn	Share	Value in EUR mn	Share	Value in EUR mn	Share
Personal income taxes and social security contributions	1354	0.8%	1321	0.8%	1287.50	0.7%
Corporate income taxes	831	2.1%	799	2.0%	766.78	2.0%
Value added taxes	1529	1.6%	1414.379	1.5%	1300.017	1.4%
Total	3714	1.2%	3534	1.1%	3354	1.1%

Table A.9. Sensitivity analysis: lost sales for Italian manufacturing industries, 2013

Sector	Scenario 1		Scenario 2		Scenario 3	
	Value in EUR mn	Share of sales	Value in EUR mn	Share of sales	Value in EUR mn	Share of sales
Food, beverages and tobacco	4160.97	3.3%	4009.95	3.2%	3858.93	3.1%
Chemical and allied products	246.82	0.7%	230.26	0.7%	213.69	0.6%
Pharmaceutical and medicinal chemical products	20.94	0.1%	19.18	0.1%	17.42	0.1%
Perfumery and cosmetics	468.62	8.5%	444.10	8.0%	419.58	7.6%
Textiles and other intermediate products	3196.46	2.8%	2895.66	2.5%	2594.85	2.2%
Clothing, footwear, leather and related products	3534.91	8.8%	3253.56	8.2%	2972.21	7.5%
Watches and jewellery	1255.37	6.9%	1135.84	6.2%	1016.31	5.6%
Non-metallic mineral products	400.74	1.4%	363.92	1.3%	327.10	1.1%
Basic metals and fabricated metal products	2948.71	2.2%	2796.36	2.0%	2644.00	1.9%
Electronic, electrical, and optical products, scientific instruments	4646.64	8.0%	4487.05	7.7%	4327.46	7.4%
Machinery, industrial equipment; computers and peripheral equipment	2626.64	1.9%	2494.42	1.8%	2362.21	1.7%
Motor vehicles and motorcycles	920.89	2.0%	826.64	1.8%	732.40	1.6%
Household cultural and recreation goods	318.54	7.6%	298.63	7.1%	278.71	6.6%
Furniture and other manufacturing n.e.c	344.77	1.2%	313.09	1.1%	281.41	1.0%
Total manufacturing sector	25091.02	3.1%	23568.65	2.9%	22046.28	2.7%

Table A.10. Sensitivity analysis: lost jobs in Italian manufacturing industries, 2013

Sector	Scenario 1		Scenario 2		Scenario 3	
	Number	Share	Number	Share	Number	Share
Food, beverages and tobacco	8510	2.0%	8201	1.9%	7893	1.8%
Chemical and allied products	328	0.4%	306	0.3%	284	0.3%
Pharmaceutical and medicinal chemical products	38	0.1%	35	0.1%	32	0.1%
Perfumery and cosmetics	673	4.4%	638	4.2%	603	4.0%
Textiles and other intermediate products	11228	1.8%	10171	1.6%	9114	1.4%
Clothing, footwear, leather and related products	17407	5.1%	16021	4.7%	14636	4.3%
Watches and jewellery	1091	3.3%	987	3.0%	883	2.7%
Non-metallic mineral products	1916	0.9%	1740	0.9%	1564	0.8%
Basic metals and fabricated metal products	7589	1.1%	7197	1.1%	6805	1.0%
Electronic, electrical, and optical products, scientific instruments	7176	4.0%	6929	3.9%	6683	3.7%
Machinery, industrial equipment; computers and peripheral equipment	5210	0.8%	4948	0.8%	4686	0.7%
Motor vehicles and motorcycles	1516	0.9%	1361	0.8%	1206	0.7%
Household cultural and recreation goods	429	4.0%	402	3.8%	375	3.5%
Furniture and other manufacturing n.e.c	1204	0.5%	1093	0.5%	983	0.4%
Total manufacturing sector	64316	2.4%	60031	2.2%	55747	2.0%

Table A.11. Sensitivity analysis: public revenue losses due to infringements of Italian IPR, 2013

Tax type	Scenario 1		Scenario 2		Scenario 3	
	Value in EUR mn	Share	Value in EUR mn	Share	Value in EUR mn	Share
Personal income taxes and social security contributions	2616.9	1.5%	2446.9	1.4%	2281.0	1.2%
Corporate income taxes	1730.9	4.2%	1650.6	4.0%	1570.4	3.8%
Value added taxes	1508.6	1.6%	1293.8	1.4%	1079.0	1.1%
Total	5856.4	1.9%	5391.4	1.7%	4930.4	1.6%

References

Anti-Counterfeiting Group (2007), *Consumer survey*, commisioned from independent survey specialists, http://www.wipo.int/ip-outreach/en/tools/research/details.jsp?id=691.

Eurostat (2018), *Structural Business Statistics (SBS) and Global Business Activities*, Eurostat, http://ec.europa.eu/eurostat/web/structural-business-statistics.

Hald, A. (1952), *Statistical Theory with Engineering Applications*, John Wiley and Sons, New York.

OECD (2018), *OECD Tax Database*, OECD, Paris, http://www.oecd.org/tax/tax-policy/tax-database.htm.

OECD/EUIPO (2016), *Trade in Counterfeit and Pirated Goods: Mapping the Economic Impact*, OECD Publishing, Paris, http://dx.doi.org/10.1787/9789264252653-en.

Tom, G. et al. (1998), "Consumer demand for counterfeit goods", *Psychology & Marketing*, Vol. 15/5, pp. 405-421.

UN Trade Statistics (2017), *Harmonized commodity description and coding systems (HS)*, United Nations, Geneva, https://unstats.un.org/unsd/tradekb/Knowledgebase/50018/Harmonized-Commodity-Description-and-Coding-Systems-HS.

Verbeek, M. (2008), *A guide to modern econometrics*, John Wiley & Sons, New York.

WIPO (2017), "PATENTSCOPE Database: International and National Patent Collection", https://patentscope.wipo.int/search/en/search.jsf (accessed on 26 November 2018).

WIPO (2016), "Global Brand Database", http://www.wipo.int/branddb/en/ (accessed on 24 November 2018).

Yoo, B. and S. Lee (2009), "Buy genuine luxury fashion products or counterfeits?", *Advances in Consumer Research*, Vol. 36, pp. 280-286.

Notes

[1] The purposes of this exercise were: i) to assess the proportion of consumers who, given that choice, would choose to purchase the counterfeit item; ii) to determine their product attitudes; and iii) to obtain demographic characteristics.

[2] Note that 39% of the sample stated that they had knowingly purchased counterfeit products; 61% stated that they have never knowingly purchased counterfeit goods.

[3] The remaining share of consumers was split as follows: 45% of fake buyers would not have bought the corresponding legitimate item and 16% would have bought another fake item in the case of clothing and footwear. These figures are 39% and 33%, respectively, in the case of watches; and 37% and 14%, respectively, in the case of fragrances. No additional investigation about potential price differences between genuine and fake offerings was undertaken.

Annex B. Additional tables

Table B.1. Likelihood of economies to be the source of counterfeit and pirated imports in Italy

GTRIC-e, 2011-2013

Provenance economy	2011	2012	2013	Provenance economy	2011	2012	2013
Albania	0.292	0.271	0.390	Congo	0.071	0.063	0.116
Algeria	0.135	0.121	0.202	Cook Islands	0.000	0.000	0.000
Angola	0.073	0.064	0.118	Costa Rica	0.000	0.000	0.000
Anguilla	0.000	0.000	0.000	Côte d'Ivoire	0.000	0.000	0.000
Antigua and Barbuda	0.000	0.000	0.000	Croatia	0.068	0.060	0.112
Argentina	0.000	0.000	0.000	Cuba	0.000	0.000	0.000
Armenia	0.000	0.000	0.000	Curaçao	0.000	0.000	0.000
Aruba	0.000	0.000	0.000	Cyprus*	0.000	0.000	0.000
Australia	0.071	0.063	0.116	Czech Republic	0.000	0.000	0.000
Austria	0.000	0.000	0.000	Democratic People's Republic of Korea	0.000	0.000	0.000
Azerbaijan	0.000	0.000	0.000	Democratic Republic of the Congo	0.000	0.000	0.000
Bahamas	0.000	0.000	0.000	Denmark	0.000	0.000	0.000
Bahrain	0.000	0.000	0.000	Djibouti	0.000	0.000	0.000
Bangladesh	0.224	0.206	0.312	Dominica	0.000	0.000	0.000
Barbados	0.000	0.000	0.000	Dominican Republic	0.128	0.115	0.193
Belarus	0.000	0.000	0.000	Ecuador	0.070	0.062	0.113
Belgium	0.215	0.198	0.302	Egypt	0.221	0.203	0.308
Belize	0.000	0.000	0.000	El Salvador	0.000	0.000	0.000
Benin	0.000	0.000	0.000	Equatorial Guinea	0.000	0.000	0.000
Bermuda	0.000	0.000	0.000	Eritrea	0.000	0.000	0.000
Bhutan	0.000	0.000	0.000	Estonia	0.000	0.000	0.000
Bolivia	0.000	0.000	0.000	Ethiopia	0.000	0.000	0.000
Bosnia and Herzegovina	0.000	0.000	0.000	Falkland Islands (Malvinas)	0.000	0.000	0.000
Botswana	0.000	0.000	0.000	Faroe Islands	0.000	0.000	0.000
Brazil	0.000	0.000	0.000	Fiji	0.000	0.000	0.000
British Indian Ocean Territory	0.000	0.000	0.000	Finland	0.000	0.000	0.000
British Virgin Islands	0.000	0.000	0.000	Former Yugoslav Republic of Macedonia	0.000	0.000	0.000
Brunei Darussalam	0.000	0.000	0.000	France	0.071	0.063	0.115
Bulgaria	0.800	0.782	0.866	French Polynesia	0.000	0.000	0.000
Burkina Faso	0.000	0.000	0.000	French Southern and Antarctic Lands	0.000	0.000	0.000
Burundi	0.000	0.000	0.000	Gabon	0.000	0.000	0.000
Cabo Verde	0.000	0.000	0.000	Gambia	0.000	0.000	0.000
Cambodia	0.000	0.000	0.000	Georgia	0.000	0.000	0.000
Cameroon	0.000	0.000	0.000	Germany	0.434	0.410	0.541
Canada	0.136	0.123	0.203	Ghana	0.243	0.224	0.334
Cayman Islands	0.000	0.000	0.000	Gibraltar	0.000	0.000	0.000
Central African Republic	0.000	0.000	0.000	Greece	1.000	1.000	1.000
Chad	0.000	0.000	0.000	Greenland	0.000	0.000	0.000
Chile	0.071	0.063	0.116	Grenada	0.000	0.000	0.000
China (People's Republic of)	1.000	0.999	1.000	Guam	0.000	0.000	0.000
Christmas Island	0.000	0.000	0.000	Guatemala	0.000	0.000	0.000
Cocos (Keeling) Islands	0.000	0.000	0.000	Guinea	0.000	0.000	0.000
Colombia	0.000	0.000	0.000	Guinea-Bissau	0.000	0.000	0.000
Comoros	0.000	0.000	0.000	Guyana	0.000	0.000	0.000

Table B.1. Likelihood of economies to be the source of counterfeit and pirated imports in Italy
(continued)

GTRIC-e, 2011-2013

Provenance economy	2011	2012	2013	Provenance economy	2011	2012	2013
Haiti	0.000	0.000	0.000	Mozambique	0.000	0.000	0.000
Heard Island and Mcdonald Islands	0.000	0.000	0.000	Myanmar	0.000	0.000	0.000
Holy See	0.000	0.000	0.000	Namibia	0.000	0.000	0.000
Honduras	0.069	0.061	0.113	Nauru	0.000	0.000	0.000
Hong Kong (China)	1.000	1.000	1.000	Nepal	0.000	0.000	0.000
Hungary	0.071	0.063	0.115	Netherlands	0.213	0.196	0.299
Iceland	0.000	0.000	0.000	New Caledonia	0.000	0.000	0.000
India	0.240	0.221	0.330	New Zealand	0.000	0.000	0.000
Indonesia	0.147	0.133	0.218	Nicaragua	0.000	0.000	0.000
Iran	0.068	0.060	0.112	Niger	0.000	0.000	0.000
Iraq	0.000	0.000	0.000	Nigeria	0.059	0.052	0.099
Ireland	0.000	0.000	0.000	Niue	0.000	0.000	0.000
Israel	0.000	0.000	0.000	Northern Mariana Islands	0.000	0.000	0.000
Italy	0.211	0.194	0.297	Norway	0.000	0.000	0.000
Jamaica	0.000	0.000	0.000	Oman	0.000	0.000	0.000
Japan	0.068	0.060	0.112	Pakistan	0.536	0.511	0.640
Jordan	0.000	0.000	0.000	Palestinian Authority*	0.000	0.000	0.000
Kazakhstan	0.000	0.000	0.000	Panama	0.000	0.000	0.000
Kenya	0.000	0.000	0.000	Papua New Guinea	0.000	0.000	0.000
Kiribati	0.000	0.000	0.000	Paraguay	0.171	0.156	0.248
Korea	0.073	0.065	0.119	Peru	0.410	0.386	0.516
Kuwait	0.000	0.000	0.000	Philippines	0.541	0.517	0.645
Kyrgyzstan	0.000	0.000	0.000	Pitcairn	0.000	0.000	0.000
Lao People's Democratic Republic	0.000	0.000	0.000	Poland	0.000	0.000	0.000
Latvia	0.000	0.000	0.000	Portugal	0.154	0.139	0.226
Lebanon	0.174	0.159	0.252	Qatar	0.071	0.063	0.116
Lesotho	0.000	0.000	0.000	Romania	0.071	0.063	0.116
Liberia	0.000	0.000	0.000	Russia	0.071	0.063	0.115
Libya	0.223	0.204	0.310	Rwanda	0.000	0.000	0.000
Lithuania	0.000	0.000	0.000	Saint Helena	0.000	0.000	0.000
Luxembourg	0.060	0.053	0.099	Saint Kitts and Nevis	0.000	0.000	0.000
Macau (China)	0.000	0.000	0.000	Saint Lucia	0.000	0.000	0.000
Madagascar	0.000	0.000	0.000	Saint Pierre and Miquelon	0.000	0.000	0.000
Malawi	0.000	0.000	0.000	Saint Vincent and the Grenadines	0.000	0.000	0.000
Malaysia	0.264	0.244	0.358	Samoa	0.000	0.000	0.000
Maldives	0.000	0.000	0.000	Sao Tome and Principe	0.000	0.000	0.000
Mali	0.000	0.000	0.000	Saudi Arabia	0.000	0.000	0.000
Malta	0.253	0.234	0.346	Senegal	1.000	1.000	1.000
Marshall Islands	0.000	0.000	0.000	Serbia	0.000	0.000	0.000
Mauritania	0.000	0.000	0.000	Seychelles	0.000	0.000	0.000
Mauritius	0.000	0.000	0.000	Sierra Leone	0.000	0.000	0.000
Mayotte	0.000	0.000	0.000	Singapore	0.639	0.615	0.733
Mexico	0.059	0.052	0.099	Slovak Republic	0.000	0.000	0.000
Micronesia	0.000	0.000	0.000	Slovenia	0.756	0.736	0.832
Moldova	0.000	0.000	0.000	Solomon Islands	0.000	0.000	0.000
Mongolia	0.000	0.000	0.000	Somalia	0.000	0.000	0.000
Montenegro	0.000	0.000	0.000	South Africa	0.062	0.055	0.103
Morocco	0.743	0.722	0.821	Spain	0.138	0.125	0.206

Table B.1. Likelihood of economies to be the source of counterfeit and pirated imports in Italy *(end)*

GTRIC-e, 2011-2013

Provenance economy	2011	2012	2013	Provenance economy	2011	2012	2013
Sri Lanka	0.069	0.061	0.113	Turkey	0.705	0.683	0.790
Sudan	0.000	0.000	0.000	Turkmenistan	0.000	0.000	0.000
Suriname	0.000	0.000	0.000	Turks and Caicos Islands	0.000	0.000	0.000
Swaziland	0.000	0.000	0.000	Tuvalu	0.000	0.000	0.000
Sweden	0.000	0.000	0.000	Uganda	0.000	0.000	0.000
Switzerland	0.229	0.210	0.317	Ukraine	0.059	0.052	0.098
Syrian Arab Republic	0.367	0.343	0.471	United Arab Emirates	0.955	0.949	0.975
Tajikistan	0.000	0.000	0.000	United Kingdom	0.214	0.196	0.300
Tanzania	0.000	0.000	0.000	United States	0.209	0.191	0.294
Thailand	0.306	0.285	0.406	Venezuela	0.069	0.061	0.112
Timor-Leste	0.000	0.000	0.000	Viet Nam	0.231	0.212	0.320
Togo	0.000	0.000	0.000	Wallis and Futuna	0.000	0.000	0.000
Tokelau	0.000	0.000	0.000	Yemen	0.000	0.000	0.000
Tonga	0.000	0.000	0.000	Zambia	0.000	0.000	0.000
Trinidad and Tobago	0.000	0.000	0.000	Zimbabwe	0.000	0.000	0.000
Tunisia	0.851	0.836	0.905				

Notes: A high GTRIC-e score indicates that an economy is highly prone to be a source of counterfeit products sold in Italy, either in absolute terms or as a share of Italian imports.

Note by Turkey: The information in this document with reference to "Cyprus" relates to the southern part of the Island. There is no single authority representing both Turkish and Greek Cypriot people on the Island. Turkey recognises the Turkish Republic of Northern Cyprus (TRNC). Until a lasting and equitable solution is found within the context of the United Nations, Turkey shall preserve its position concerning the "Cyprus issue".

Note by all the European Union Member States of the OECD and the European Union: The Republic of Cyprus is recognised by all members of the United Nations with the exception of Turkey. The information in this document relates to the area under the effective control of the Government of the Republic of Cyprus.

The statistical data for Israel are supplied by and under the responsibility of the relevant Israeli authorities. The use of such data by the OECD is without prejudice to the status of the Golan Heights, East Jerusalem and Israeli settlements in the West Bank under the terms of international law.

Table B.2. Likelihood of product categories to be affected by counterfeiting and piracy

GTRIC-p, 2011-2013

Product category (HS codes)	2011	2012	2013
Foodstuffs (02-21)	0.238	0.233	0.194
Tobacco (24)	1.000	1.000	1.000
Pharmaceutical products (30)	0.283	0.276	0.234
Tanning or dyeing extracts (32)	0.390	0.382	0.333
Perfumery and cosmetics (33)	0.914	0.911	0.888
Soap; albuminoidal substances; glues; explosives (34-37)	0.179	0.174	0.142
Miscellaneous chemical products (38)	0.157	0.153	0.124
Plastic and articles thereof (39)	0.395	0.388	0.339
Rubber and article thereof (40)	0.229	0.223	0.186
Articles of leather; handbags (42)	1.000	1.000	0.999
Pulp and paper (47/48)	0.350	0.343	0.296
Printed articles (49)	0.879	0.875	0.845
Carpets and rugs (57)	0.078	0.076	0.058
Finishing of textiles (58)	0.158	0.153	0.124
Clothing and accessories, not knitted or crocheted (62/65)	0.458	0.451	0.400
Clothing, knitted or crocheted (61)	0.993	0.992	0.989
Other made-up textile articles (63)	0.186	0.181	0.148
Footwear (64)	0.970	0.968	0.957
Glass and glassware (70)	0.196	0.191	0.157
Jewellery (71)	0.506	0.498	0.446
Iron and steel; and articles thereof (72/73)	0.315	0.309	0.264
Copper; nickel; aluminium; lead; zinc; tin;and articles thereof (74-81)	0.078	0.075	0.058
Tools and cutlery of base metal (82)	0.257	0.251	0.211
Miscellaneous articles of base metal (83)	0.165	0.160	0.130
Machinery and mechanical appliances (84)	0.374	0.367	0.319
Electrical machinery and electronics (85)	0.846	0.841	0.807
Vehicles (87)	0.535	0.528	0.475
Optical; photographic; medical apparatus (90)	0.870	0.866	0.835
Watches (91)	1.000	1.000	1.000
Furnitures (94)	0.193	0.188	0.154
Toys and games (95)	0.987	0.987	0.981
Miscellaneous manufactured articles (66/67/96)	1.000	1.000	1.000

Notes: A high GTRIC-p score signals a product category that is more likely to be counterfeit – that is to say, it contains high euro values for counterfeit products, or a large share of Italian sales in that product category is counterfeit. Figures in parenthesis are Harmonized System (HS) codes as defined by the United Nations Trade Statistics (UN Trade Statistics, 2017). GTRIC-p values are zero for HS categories non-displayed in this table.

Table B.3. Estimates of counterfeit and pirated imports in Italy by product category, 2011-2013

Unit	Value in EUR mn			Share of imports within the category		
HS category	2011	2012	2013	2011	2012	2013
Foodstuffs (02-21)	464.0	418.0	481.0	1.5%	1.3%	1.5%
Tobacco (24)	138.0	127.0	158.0	6.2%	5.8%	7.7%
Pharmaceutical products (30)	257.0	246.0	297.0	1.6%	1.5%	1.9%
Tanning or dyeing extracts (32)	70.3	61.6	71.5	3.2%	3.0%	3.5%
Perfumery and cosmetics (33)	106.0	96.3	134.0	4.6%	4.2%	5.8%
Soap; albuminoidal substances; glues; explosives (34-37)	27.2	24.1	26.8	1.3%	1.2%	1.3%
Miscellaneous chemical products (38)	48.4	45.4	48.6	0.9%	0.8%	1.0%
Plastic and articles thereof (39)	466.0	408.0	476.0	3.0%	2.7%	3.1%
Rubber and article thereof (40)	81.3	64.2	68.1	1.7%	1.6%	1.7%
Articles of leather; handbags (42)	359.0	346.0	352.0	15.5%	14.8%	15.3%
Pulp and paper (47/48)	122.0	99.7	115.0	1.8%	1.6%	1.9%
Printed articles (49)	49.6	47.1	54.7	8.0%	7.9%	9.6%
Carpets and rugs (57)	1.4	1.2	1.2	0.7%	0.7%	0.7%
Finishing of textiles (58)	4.2	4.0	3.5	2.0%	1.9%	1.6%
Clothing, knitted or crocheted (61)	784.0	675.0	725.0	12.3%	11.5%	12.7%
Clothing and accessories, not knitted or crocheted (62/65)	425.0	359.0	328.0	6.5%	6.0%	5.8%
Other made-up textile articles (63)	24.8	20.6	20.0	2.5%	2.4%	2.2%
Footwear (64)	472.0	430.0	495.0	9.7%	9.5%	10.8%
Glass and glassware (70)	29.1	24.7	24.1	1.8%	1.7%	1.6%
Jewellery (71)	256.0	252.0	283.0	2.9%	2.5%	3.6%
Iron and steel; and articles thereof (72/73)	493.0	365.0	392.0	2.2%	2.0%	2.2%
Copper; nickel; aluminium; lead; zinc; articles thereof (74-81)	86.4	68.8	64.2	0.6%	0.6%	0.5%
Tools and cutlery of base metal (82)	30.5	25.4	27.6	2.5%	2.2%	2.4%
Miscellaneous articles of base metal (83)	21.6	18.9	17.6	1.8%	1.6%	1.5%
Machinery and mechanical appliances (84)	1130.0	1050.0	1080.0	3.5%	3.4%	3.5%
Electrical machinery and electronics (85)	3120.0	2230.0	2260.0	9.6%	8.3%	9.3%
Vehicles (87)	1270.0	897.0	1020.0	4.0%	3.6%	4.2%
Optical; photographic; medical apparatus (90)	668.0	629.0	781.0	7.4%	7.3%	9.0%
Watches (91)	102.0	101.0	128.0	8.7%	7.8%	9.8%
Furnitures (94)	63.8	56.6	51.4	2.3%	2.2%	2.0%
Toys and games (95)	312.0	262.0	247.0	14.3%	13.4%	14.3%
Miscellaneous manufactured articles (66/67/96)	115.0	109.0	126.0	14.2%	11.8%	13.4%

Notes: Figures in parenthesis are Harmonized System (HS) codes as defined by the United Nations Trade Statistics (UN Trade Statistics, 2017). Values are zero for HS categories non-displayed in this table.

Table B.4. Likelihood of economies to import counterfeit products infringing Italian IPR

GTRIC-e for destination economies, 2011-2013

Destination economy	2011	2012	2013	Destination economy	2011	2012	2013
Afghanistan	0.000	0.000	0.000	Congo	0.836	0.836	0.835
Albania	0.670	0.670	0.668	Cook Islands	0.000	0.000	0.000
Algeria	0.289	0.289	0.288	Costa Rica	0.000	0.000	0.000
American Samoa	0.000	0.000	0.000	Côte d'Ivoire	0.000	0.000	0.000
Andorra	0.000	0.000	0.000	Croatia	0.204	0.204	0.203
Angola	0.000	0.000	0.000	Cuba	0.000	0.000	0.000
Anguilla	0.000	0.000	0.000	Curaçao	0.000	0.000	0.000
Antigua and Barbuda	0.000	0.000	0.000	Cyprus*	0.485	0.485	0.483
Argentina	0.554	0.554	0.552	Czech Republic	0.883	0.883	0.882
Armenia	0.000	0.000	0.000	Democratic People's Republic of Korea	0.000	0.000	0.000
Aruba	0.000	0.000	0.000	Democratic Republic of the Congo	1.000	1.000	1.000
Australia	0.198	0.198	0.196	Denmark	0.310	0.310	0.308
Austria	0.290	0.290	0.288	Djibouti	0.397	0.397	0.396
Azerbaijan	0.000	0.000	0.000	Dominica	0.000	0.000	0.000
Bahamas	0.146	0.146	0.145	Dominican Republic	0.162	0.162	0.161
Bahrain	0.000	0.000	0.000	Ecuador	0.000	0.000	0.000
Bangladesh	0.000	0.000	0.000	Egypt	0.000	0.000	0.000
Barbados	0.000	0.000	0.000	El Salvador	0.164	0.164	0.163
Belarus	0.000	0.000	0.000	Equatorial Guinea	0.000	0.000	0.000
Belgium	0.416	0.416	0.414	Eritrea	0.000	0.000	0.000
Belize	0.000	0.000	0.000	Estonia	0.308	0.308	0.307
Benin	0.000	0.000	0.000	Ethiopia	0.000	0.000	0.000
Bermuda	0.000	0.000	0.000	Falkland Islands (Malvinas)	0.000	0.000	0.000
Bhutan	0.000	0.000	0.000	Faroe Islands	0.000	0.000	0.000
Bolivia	0.000	0.000	0.000	Fiji	0.000	0.000	0.000
Bonaire	0.000	0.000	0.000	Finland	0.537	0.537	0.535
Bosnia and Herzegovina	0.354	0.354	0.353	Former Yugoslav Republic of Macedonia	0.439	0.439	0.438
Botswana	0.000	0.000	0.000	France	0.330	0.330	0.329
Bouvet Island	0.000	0.000	0.000	French Polynesia	0.000	0.000	0.000
Brazil	0.147	0.147	0.146	French Southern and Antartic Lands	0.000	0.000	0.000
British Virgin Islands	0.000	0.000	0.000	Gabon	0.000	0.000	0.000
Brunei Darussalam	0.000	0.000	0.000	Gambia	0.000	0.000	0.000
Bulgaria	0.719	0.719	0.717	Georgia	0.000	0.000	0.000
Burkina Faso	0.000	0.000	0.000	Germany	0.363	0.363	0.362
Burundi	0.000	0.000	0.000	Ghana	0.155	0.155	0.154
Cabo Verde	0.000	0.000	0.000	Gibraltar	0.000	0.000	0.000
Cambodia	0.000	0.000	0.000	Greece	0.000	0.000	0.000
Cameroon	0.000	0.000	0.000	Greenland	0.000	0.000	0.000
Canada	0.000	0.000	0.000	Grenada	0.000	0.000	0.000
Cayman Islands	0.000	0.000	0.000	Guam	0.000	0.000	0.000
Central African Republic	0.000	0.000	0.000	Guatemala	0.000	0.000	0.000
Chad	0.000	0.000	0.000	Guinea	0.878	0.878	0.877
Chile	0.568	0.568	0.566	Guinea-Bissau	0.000	0.000	0.000
China (People's Republic of)	0.285	0.285	0.283	Guyana	0.000	0.000	0.000
Christmas Island	0.000	0.000	0.000	Haiti	0.000	0.000	0.000
Cocos (Keeling) Islands	0.000	0.000	0.000	Holy See	0.000	0.000	0.000
Colombia	0.389	0.389	0.388	Honduras	0.000	0.000	0.000
Comoros	0.000	0.000	0.000	Hong Kong (China)	0.000	0.000	0.000

Table B.4. Likelihood of economies to import counterfeit products infringing Italian IPR *(continued)*

GTRIC-e for destination economies, 2011-2013

Destination economy	2011	2012	2013	Destination economy	2011	2012	2013
Hungary	0.659	0.659	0.657	Netherlands	0.423	0.423	0.421
Iceland	0.000	0.000	0.000	New Caledonia	0.000	0.000	0.000
India	0.000	0.000	0.000	New Zealand	0.000	0.000	0.000
Indonesia	0.000	0.000	0.000	Nicaragua	0.000	0.000	0.000
Iran	0.000	0.000	0.000	Niger	0.000	0.000	0.000
Iraq	0.000	0.000	0.000	Nigeria	0.000	0.000	0.000
Ireland	0.432	0.432	0.431	Niue	0.000	0.000	0.000
Israel	0.271	0.271	0.269	Norfolk Island	0.000	0.000	0.000
Jamaica	0.000	0.000	0.000	Northern Mariana Islands	0.000	0.000	0.000
Japan	0.474	0.474	0.472	Norway	0.000	0.000	0.000
Jordan	0.000	0.000	0.000	Oman	0.000	0.000	0.000
Kazakhstan	0.000	0.000	0.000	Pakistan	0.000	0.000	0.000
Kenya	0.000	0.000	0.000	Palau	0.000	0.000	0.000
Kiribati	0.000	0.000	0.000	Palestinian Authority*	0.000	0.000	0.000
Korea	0.146	0.146	0.145	Panama	0.000	0.000	0.000
Kuwait	0.994	0.994	0.994	Papua New Guinea	0.000	0.000	0.000
Kyrgyzstan	0.000	0.000	0.000	Paraguay	1.000	1.000	1.000
Lao People's Democratic Republic	0.000	0.000	0.000	Peru	0.000	0.000	0.000
Latvia	0.529	0.529	0.527	Philippines	0.000	0.000	0.000
Lebanon	0.000	0.000	0.000	Pitcairn	0.000	0.000	0.000
Lesotho	0.000	0.000	0.000	Poland	0.284	0.284	0.282
Liberia	0.000	0.000	0.000	Portugal	0.833	0.833	0.832
Libya	0.150	0.150	0.149	Qatar	0.000	0.000	0.000
Lithuania	0.286	0.286	0.285	Romania	0.403	0.403	0.401
Luxembourg	0.361	0.361	0.359	Russia	0.313	0.313	0.311
Macau (China)	0.000	0.000	0.000	Rwanda	0.000	0.000	0.000
Madagascar	0.000	0.000	0.000	Saint Barthélemy	0.000	0.000	0.000
Malawi	0.000	0.000	0.000	Saint Helena	0.000	0.000	0.000
Malaysia	0.000	0.000	0.000	Saint Kitts and Nevis	0.000	0.000	0.000
Maldives	0.000	0.000	0.000	Saint Lucia	0.000	0.000	0.000
Mali	0.000	0.000	0.000	Saint Pierre and Miquelon	0.000	0.000	0.000
Malta	0.345	0.345	0.343	Saint Vincent and the Grenadines	0.000	0.000	0.000
Marshall Islands	0.000	0.000	0.000	Samoa	0.000	0.000	0.000
Mauritania	0.000	0.000	0.000	San Marino	0.147	0.147	0.146
Mauritius	0.149	0.149	0.148	Sao Tome and Principe	0.000	0.000	0.000
Mayotte	0.000	0.000	0.000	Saudi Arabia	0.340	0.340	0.339
Mexico	0.146	0.146	0.145	Senegal	0.161	0.161	0.160
Micronesia	0.000	0.000	0.000	Serbia	0.290	0.290	0.289
Moldova	0.000	0.000	0.000	Seychelles	0.000	0.000	0.000
Mongolia	0.000	0.000	0.000	Sierra Leone	0.000	0.000	0.000
Montenegro	0.638	0.638	0.636	Singapore	0.000	0.000	0.000
Montserrat	0.000	0.000	0.000	Sint Maarten	0.000	0.000	0.000
Morocco	0.467	0.467	0.466	Slovak Republic	0.483	0.483	0.481
Mozambique	0.000	0.000	0.000	Slovenia	0.374	0.374	0.372
Myanmar	0.000	0.000	0.000	Solomon Islands	0.000	0.000	0.000
Namibia	0.000	0.000	0.000	Somalia	0.000	0.000	0.000
Nauru	0.000	0.000	0.000	South Africa	0.000	0.000	0.000

Table B.4. Likelihood of economies to import counterfeit products infringing Italian IPR (*end*)

GTRIC-e for destination economies, 2011-2013

Destination economy	2011	2012	2013	Destination economy	2011	2012	2013
South Sudan	0.000	0.000	0.000	Turkey	0.146	0.146	0.145
Spain	0.875	0.875	0.874	Turkmenistan	0.000	0.000	0.000
Sri Lanka	0.000	0.000	0.000	Turks and Caicos Islands	0.000	0.000	0.000
Sudan	0.408	0.408	0.406	Tuvalu	0.000	0.000	0.000
Suriname	0.000	0.000	0.000	Uganda	0.000	0.000	0.000
Swaziland	0.000	0.000	0.000	Ukraine	0.296	0.296	0.294
Sweden	0.304	0.304	0.302	United Arab Emirates	0.284	0.284	0.283
Switzerland	0.284	0.284	0.283	United Kingdom	0.619	0.619	0.617
Syrian Arab Republic	0.000	0.000	0.000	United States	0.374	0.374	0.373
Tajikistan	0.000	0.000	0.000	Uruguay	0.000	0.000	0.000
Tanzania	0.000	0.000	0.000	Uzbekistan	0.000	0.000	0.000
Thailand	0.000	0.000	0.000	Vanuatu	0.000	0.000	0.000
Timor-Leste	0.000	0.000	0.000	Venezuela	0.291	0.291	0.289
Togo	0.991	0.991	0.991	Viet Nam	0.218	0.218	0.216
Tokelau	0.000	0.000	0.000	Wallis and Futuna	0.000	0.000	0.000
Tonga	0.000	0.000	0.000	Yemen	0.174	0.174	0.173
Trinidad and Tobago	0.000	0.000	0.000	Zambia	0.000	0.000	0.000
Tunisia	0.000	0.000	0.000	Zimbabwe	0.000	0.000	0.000

Notes: A high GTRIC-e score indicates that an economy is highly prone to be a destination market for counterfeit products infringing Italian trademarks and patents, either in absolute terms or as a share of Italian sales.

Note by Turkey: The information in this document with reference to "Cyprus" relates to the southern part of the Island. There is no single authority representing both Turkish and Greek Cypriot people on the Island. Turkey recognises the Turkish Republic of Northern Cyprus (TRNC). Until a lasting and equitable solution is found within the context of the United Nations, Turkey shall preserve its position concerning the "Cyprus issue".

Note by all the European Union Member States of the OECD and the European Union: The Republic of Cyprus is recognised by all members of the United Nations with the exception of Turkey. The information in this document relates to the area under the effective control of the Government of the Republic of Cyprus.

The statistical data for Israel are supplied by and under the responsibility of the relevant Israeli authorities. The use of such data by the OECD is without prejudice to the status of the Golan Heights, East Jerusalem and Israeli settlements in the West Bank under the terms of international law.

Table B.5. Likelihood that product categories will be targeted by infringements of Italian IP

GTRIC-p for goods infringing Italian IPR, 2011-2013

HS category	2011	2012	2013
Foodstuffs (02-21)	0.227	0.227	0.122
Tanning or dyeing extracts (32)	0.098	0.098	0.042
Perfumery and cosmetics (33)	0.997	0.997	0.990
Plastic and articles thereof (39)	0.255	0.255	0.141
Articles of leather; handbags (42)	1.000	1.000	0.999
Pulp and paper (47/48)	0.210	0.210	0.110
Printed articles (49)	0.211	0.211	0.111
Carpets and rugs (57)	0.180	0.180	0.091
Finishing of textiles (58)	0.987	0.987	0.962
Knitted or crocheted fabrics (60)	0.324	0.324	0.192
Clothing, knitted or crocheted (61)	0.988	0.988	0.965
Clothing and accessories, not knitted or crocheted (62/65)	0.996	0.996	0.986
Other made-up textile articles (63)	0.384	0.384	0.241
Footwear (64)	0.853	0.853	0.737
Glass and glassware (70)	0.299	0.299	0.173
Jewellery (71)	0.439	0.439	0.288
Iron and steel; and articles thereof (72/73)	0.104	0.104	0.046
Tools and cutlery of base metal (82)	0.272	0.272	0.154
Miscellaneous articles of base metal (83)	0.620	0.620	0.460
Machinery and mechanical appliances (84)	0.213	0.213	0.112
Electrical machinery and electronics (85)	0.320	0.320	0.189
Vehicles (87)	0.213	0.213	0.112
Optical; photographic; medical apparatus (90)	1.000	1.000	1.000
Watches (91)	1.000	1.000	1.000
Musical instruments (92)	0.098	0.098	0.042
Furniture (94)	0.099	0.099	0.043
Toys and games (95)	0.491	0.491	0.334
Miscellaneous manufactured articles (66/67/96)	0.240	0.240	0.130

Notes: A high GTRIC-p score implies either that a given product category contains high values of Italian trademarks or patents that are sensitive to global counterfeiting and piracy in absolute terms (e.g. in euros); or, that a large share of the production of goods associated with an Italian trademark or patent registered in this product category is counterfeit or pirated. Figures in parenthesis are Harmonized System (HS) codes as defined by the United Nations Trade Statistics (UN Trade Statistics, 2017). Values are zero for HS categories non-displayed in this table.

Table B.6. Correspondence between HS categories and sectors

Sector	HS category
Food, beverages and tobacco	Foodstuffs (02-21)
	Beverages (22)
	Residues from the food industries (23)
	Tobacco (24)
Chemical and allied products; except pharmaceuticals, perfumery and cosmetics	Fertilisers (31)
	Miscellaneous chemical products (38)
	Tanning or dyeing extracts (32)
	Organic and inorganic chemicals (28/29)
	Soap; albuminoidal substances; glues; explosives (34-37)

Table B.6. Correspondence between HS categories and sectors (*continued*)

Sector	HS category
Pharmaceutical and medicinal chemical products	Pharmaceutical products (30)
Perfumery and cosmetics	Perfumery and cosmetics (33)
Textiles and other intermediate products (e.g. plastics; rubbers; paper; wood)	Man-made filaments and staple fibres (54/55)
	Wadding; cordage; ropes and articles thereof (56)
	Wood and articles thereof (44)
	Other textiles n.e.c. (59)
	Cork; straw and articles thereof (45/46)
	Finishing of textiles (58)
	Pulp and paper (47/48)
	Furskins and artificial fur (43)
	Raw hides, skins and leather (41)
	Silk; wool; and other vegetable textile fibres (50-53)
	Plastic and articles thereof (39)
	Rubber and article thereof (40)
Clothing, footwear, leather and related products	Other made-up textile articles (63)
	Clothing and accessories, not knitted or crocheted (62/65)
	Clothing, knitted or crocheted (61)
	Footwear (64)
	Knitted or crocheted fabrics (60)
	Articles of leather; handbags (42)
Watches and jewellery	Jewellery (71)
	Watches (91)
Non-metallic mineral products (e.g. glass and glass products, ceramic products)	Ceramic products (69)
	Articles of stone, plaster and cement (68)
	Glass and glassware (70)
Basic metals and fabricated metal products (except machinery and equipment)	Copper; nickel; aluminium; lead; zinc; tin; and articles thereof (74-81)
	Tools and cutlery of base metal (82)
	Iron and steel; and articles thereof (72/73)
	Miscellaneous articles of base metal (83)
Electrical household appliances, electronic and telecommunications equipment	Electrical machinery and electronics (85)
	Optical; photographic; medical apparatus (90)
Machinery, industrial equipment; computers and peripheral equipment; ships and aircrafts	Railway (86)
	Aircraft (88)
	Ships (89)
	Machinery and mechanical appliances (84)
Motor vehicles and motorcycles	Vehicles (87)
Household cultural and recreation goods; including toys and games, books and musical instruments	Toys and games (95)
	Printed articles (49)
	Musical instruments (92)
Furniture, lighting equipment, carpets and other manufacturing n.e.c	Carpets and rugs (57)
	Arms and ammunition (93)
	Furniture (94)
	Miscellaneous manufactured articles (66/67/96)

Notes: Figures in parenthesis are Harmonized System (HS) codes as defined by the United Nations Trade Statistics (UN Trade Statistics, 2017[18]). "Sectors" have been built for the purpose of this study, in order to merge HS product categories, NACE C (manufacturing activities) and NACE G (wholesale and retail activities) in a unified analytical framework.

Table B.7. Correspondence between NACE C. categories and sectors

Sector	NACE Rev 2. code	NACE Rev.2 description
Food, beverages and tobacco	C1000	Manufacture of food products
	C1100	Manufacture of beverages
	C1200	Manufacture of tobacco products
Chemical and allied products; except pharmaceuticals, perfumery and cosmetics	C2011	Manufacture of industrial gases
	C2012	Manufacture of dyes and pigments
	C2013	Manufacture of other inorganic basic chemicals
	C2014	Manufacture of other organic basic chemicals
	C2015	Manufacture of fertilisers and nitrogen compounds
	C2016	Manufacture of plastics in primary forms
	C2017	Manufacture of synthetic rubber in primary forms
	C2020	Manufacture of pesticides and other agrochemical products
	C2030	Manufacture of paints, varnishes and similar coatings printing ink and mastics
	C2041	Manufacture of soap and detergents
	C2051	Manufacture of explosives
	C2052	Manufacture of glues
	C2059	Manufacture of other chemical products n.e.c
Pharmaceutical and medicinal chemical products	C2100	Manufacture of basic pharmaceutical products and pharmaceutical preparations
Perfumery and cosmetics	C2042	Manufacture of perfumes and toilet preparation
	C2053	Manufacture of essential oils
	C2500	Manufacture of fabricated metal products
Electrical household appliances, electronic and telecommunications equipment	C2610	Manufacture of electronic components and boards
	C2630	Manufacture of communication equipment
	C2640	Manufacture of consumer electronics
	C2651	Manufacture of instruments and appliances for measuring, testing and navigation
	C2660	Manufacture of irradiation, electromedical and electrotherapeutic equipment
	C2670	Manufacture of optical instruments and photographic equipment
	C2680	Manufacture of magnetic and optical media
	C2720	Manufacture of batteries and accumulators
	C2731	Manufacture of fibre optic cables
	C2732	Manufacture of other electronic and electric wires and cables
	C2733	Manufacture of wiring devices
	C2740	Manufacture of electric lighting equipment
	C2790	Manufacture of other electrical equipment
Machinery, industrial equipment; computers and peripheral equipment; ships and aircrafts	C2620	Manufacture of computers and peripheral equipment
	C2711	Manufacture of electrical motors generators and transformers
	C2712	Manufacture of electricity distribution and control apparatus
	C2750	Manufacture of domestic appliances
	C2800	Manufacture of machinery and equipment n.e.c
	C3000	Manufacture of other transport equipment

Table B.7. Correspondence between NACE C. categories and sectors (*continued*)

Sector	NACE Rev 2. code	NACE Rev.2 description
Motor vehicles and motorcycles	C2900	Manufacture of motor vehicles
Textiles and other intermediate products (e.g. plastics; rubbers; paper; wood)	C1300	Manufacture of textiles
	C1600	Manufacture of wood and of products of wood and cork
	C1700	Manufacture of paper and paper products
	C1800	Printing and reproduction of recorded media
	C2060	Manufacture of man-made fibers
	C2200	Manufacture of rubber and plastic products
Clothing, footwear, leather and related products	C1400	Manufacture of wearing apparel
	C1500	Manufacture of leather, footwear and related products
Watches and jewellery	C2652	Manufacture of watches and clocks
	C3210	Manufacture of jewellery bijouterie and related articles
Basic metals and fabricated metal products (except machinery and equipment)	C2400	Manufacture of basic metals
	C2500	Manufacture of fabricated metal products
Non-metallic mineral products (e.g. glass and glass products, ceramic products)	C2300	Manufacture of other non-metallic mineral products
Machinery, industrial equipment; computers and peripheral equipment; ships and aircrafts	C2620	Manufacture of computers and peripheral equipment
	C2711	Manufacture of electrical motors generators and transformers
	C2712	Manufacture of electricity distribution and control apparatus
	C2750	Manufacture of domestic appliances
	C2800	Manufacture of machinery and equipment n.e.c
	C3000	Manufacture of other transport equipment
Household cultural and recreation goods; including toys and games, books and musical instruments	C3220	Manufacture of musical instruments
	C3230	Manufacture of sports goods
	C3240	Manufacture of games and toys
Motor vehicles and motorcycles	C2900	Manufacture of motor vehicles
Furniture, lighting equipment, carpets and other manufacturing n.e.c	C3100	Manufacture of furniture
	C3250	Manufacture of medical and dental instruments and supplies
	C3290	Manufacture n.e.c

Notes: NACE C is the statistical classification of economic activities for manufacturing industries in the European Community. It is a four-digit classification, which provides the framework for collecting and presenting a large range of statistical data according to economic activity in the fields of economic statistics (e.g. production, employment and national accounts) and in other statistical domains developed within the European statistical system (ESS). For additional information, see http://ec.europa.eu/eurostat/statistics-explained/index.php/Main_Page. "Sectors" have been built for the purpose of this study, in order to merge HS product categories, NACE C (manufacturing activities) and NACE G (wholesale and retail activities) in a unified analytical framework.

Table B.8. Correspondence between NACE G. categories and sectors

Sector	NACE code	NACE description
Food, beverages and tobacco	G4617	Agents involved in the sale of food, beverages and tobacco
	G4723	Retail sale of fish, crustaceans and molluscs in specialised stores
	G4638	Wholesale of other food, including fish, crustaceans and molluscs
	G4634	Wholesale of beverages
	G4721	Retail sale of fruit and vegetables in specialised stores
	G4726	Retail sale of tobacco products in specialised stores
	G4632	Wholesale of meat and meat products
	G4633	Wholesale of dairy products, eggs and edible oils and fats
	G4635	Wholesale of tobacco products
	G4729	Other retail sale of food in specialised stores
	G4781	Retail sale via stalls and markets of food, beverages and tobacco products
	G4631	Wholesale of fruit and vegetables
	G4636	Wholesale of sugar and chocolate and sugar confectionery
	G4724	Retail sale of bread, cakes, flour confectionery and sugar confectionery in specialised stores
	G4722	Retail sale of meat and meat products in specialised stores
	G4637	Wholesale of coffee, tea, cocoa and spices
	G4639	Non-specialised wholesale of food, beverages and tobacco
	G4711	Retail sale in non-specialised stores with food, beverages or tobacco predominating
	G4725	Retail sale of beverages in specialised stores
Chemical and allied products; except pharmaceuticals, perfumery and cosmetics	G4675	Wholesale of chemical products
Pharmaceutical and medicinal chemical products	G4646	Wholesale of pharmaceutical goods
Perfumery and cosmetics	G4775	Retail sale of cosmetic and toilet articles in specialised stores
	G4645	Wholesale of perfume and cosmetics
Textiles and other intermediate products (e.g. plastics; rubbers; paper; wood)	G4676	Wholesale of other intermediate products
	G4751	Retail sale of textiles in specialised stores
	G4641	Wholesale of textiles
	G4673	Wholesale of wood, construction materials and sanitary equipment
Clothing, footwear, leather and related products	G4771	Retail sale of clothing in specialised stores
	G4782	Retail sale via stalls and markets of textiles, clothing and footwear
	G4642	Wholesale of clothing and footwear
	G4616	Agents involved in the sale of textiles, clothing, fur, footwear and leather goods
	G4773	Dispensing chemist in specialised stores
	G4772	Retail sale of footwear and leather goods in specialised stores
Watches and jewellery	G4648	Wholesale of watches and jewellery
	G4777	Retail sale of watches and jewellery in specialised stores

Table B.8. Correspondence between NACE G. categories and sectors (*continued*)

Sector	NACE code	NACE description
Non-metallic mineral products (e.g. glass and glass products, ceramic products)	G4752	Retail sale of hardware, paints and glass in specialised stores
	G4644	Wholesale of china and glassware and cleaning materials
Basic metals and fabricated metal products (except machinery and equipment)	G4613	Agents involved in the sale of timber and building materials
	G4672	Wholesale of metals and metal ores
	G4677	Wholesale of waste and scrap
	G4674	Wholesale of hardware, plumbing and heating equipment and supplies
Electrical household appliances, electronic and telecommunications equipment	G4743	Retail sale of audio and video equipment in specialised stores
	G4742	Retail sale of telecommunications equipment in specialised stores
	G4774	Retail sale of medical and orthopaedic goods in specialised stores
	G4754	Retail sale of electrical household appliances in specialised stores
	G4652	Wholesale of electronic and telecommunications equipment and parts
	G4643	Wholesale of electrical household appliances
Machinery, industrial equipment; computers and peripheral equipment; ships and aircrafts	G4614	Agents involved in the sale of machinery, industrial equipment, ships and aircraft
	G4651	Wholesale of computers, computer peripheral equipment and software
	G4661	Wholesale of agricultural machinery, equipment and supplies
	G4663	Wholesale of mining, construction and civil engineering machinery
	G4666	Wholesale of other office machinery and equipment
	G4741	Retail sale of computers, peripheral units and software in specialised stores
	G4669	Wholesale of other machinery and equipment
	G4662	Wholesale of machine tools
	G4664	Wholesale of machinery for the textile industry and of sewing and knitting machines
Motor vehicles and motorcycles	G4511	Sale of cars and light motor vehicles
	G4540	Sale, maintenance and repair of motorcycles and related parts and accessories
	G4520	Maintenance and repair of motor vehicles
	G4532	Retail trade of motor vehicle parts and accessories
	G4531	Wholesale trade of motor vehicle parts and accessories
	G4519	Sale of other motor vehicles

Table B.8. Correspondence between NACE G. categories and sectors (*end*)

Sector	NACE code	NACE description
Household cultural and recreation goods; including toys and games, books and musical instruments	G4764	Retail sale of sporting equipment in specialised stores
	G4763	Retail sale of music and video recordings in specialised stores
	G4649	Wholesale of other household goods
	G4765	Retail sale of games and toys in specialised stores
	G4761	Retail sale of books in specialised stores
	G4762	Retail sale of newspapers and stationery in specialised stores
Furniture, lighting equipment, carpets and other manufacturing n.e.c	G4690	Non-specialised wholesale trade
	G4665	Wholesale of office furniture
	G4719	Other retail sale in non-specialised stores
	G4753	Retail sale of carpets, rugs, wall and floor coverings in specialised stores
	G4759	Retail sale of furniture, lighting equipment and other household articles in specia- lised stores
	G4615	Agents involved in the sale of furniture, household goods, hardware and iron- mongery
	G4647	Wholesale of furniture, carpets and lighting equipment
	G4778	Other retail sale of new goods in specialised stores

Notes: NACE is the statistical classification of economic activities for wholesale and retail industries in the European Community. It is a four-digit classification, which provides the framework for collecting and presenting a large range of statistical data according to economic activity in the fields of economic statistics (e.g. production, employment and national accounts) and in other statistical domains developed within the European statistical system (ESS). For additional information, see http://ec.europa.eu/eurostat/statistics-explained/index.php/Main_Page. "Sectors" have been built for the purpose of this study, in order to merge HS product categories, NACE C (manufacturing activities) and NACE G (wholesale and retail activities) in a unified analytical framework.

References

Censis (2012), *Dimensions, Features and Future information on counterfeiting, Final Report*, http://www.uibm.gov.it/iperico/home/2012_Studio_Fondazione_Censis_EN.pdf.

DGLC-UIBM (2017), *IPERICO database*, Directorate-General for the Fight against Counterfeiting – Italian Patent and Trademark Office, Roma, http://www.uibm.gov.it/iperico/home/.

EUIPO (2017), *The European Citizens and Intellectual Property Perception, Awareness and Behaviour*, European Union Intellectual Property Office.

OECD/EUIPO (2017), *Mapping the Real Routes of Trade in Fake Goods*, OECD Publishing, Paris, http://dx.doi.org/10.1787/9789264278349-en.

UN Trade Statistics (2017), *Comtrade Database*, United Nations, Geneva, https://comtrade.un.org/.

ORGANISATION FOR ECONOMIC CO-OPERATION AND DEVELOPMENT

The OECD is a unique forum where governments work together to address the economic, social and environmental challenges of globalisation. The OECD is also at the forefront of efforts to understand and to help governments respond to new developments and concerns, such as corporate governance, the information economy and the challenges of an ageing population. The Organisation provides a setting where governments can compare policy experiences, seek answers to common problems, identify good practice and work to co-ordinate domestic and international policies.

The OECD member countries are: Australia, Austria, Belgium, Canada, Chile, Colombia, the Czech Republic, Denmark, Estonia, Finland, France, Germany, Greece, Hungary, Iceland, Ireland, Israel, Italy, Japan, Korea, Latvia, Lithuania, Luxembourg, Mexico, the Netherlands, New Zealand, Norway, Poland, Portugal, the Slovak Republic, Slovenia, Spain, Sweden, Switzerland, Turkey, the United Kingdom and the United States. The European Union takes part in the work of the OECD.

OECD Publishing disseminates widely the results of the Organisation's statistics gathering and research on economic, social and environmental issues, as well as the conventions, guidelines and standards agreed by its members.

OECD PUBLISHING, 2, rue André-Pascal, 75775 PARIS CEDEX 16
(42 2018 29 1 P) ISBN 978-92-64-30241-9 – 2018

www.ingramcontent.com/pod-product-compliance
Lightning Source LLC
LaVergne TN
LVHW081415110826
845149LV00010B/1752